The Art of C Programming

D1596445

Robin Jones   Ian Stewart

The Art of
C Programming

With 42 Illustrations

Springer-Verlag
New York Berlin Heidelberg
London Paris Tokyo

Robin Jones
Computer Unit
South Kent College of
 Technology
Folkestone CT20 2NA
England

Ian Stewart
Mathematics Institute
University of Warwick
Coventry CV4 7AL
England

The illustrations by Sir John Tenniel that decorate all chapters except Appendix 2 are reproduced from *Alice's Adventures in Wonderland* and *Through the Looking Glass* by Lewis Carroll, with the permission of the publishers, MacMillan & Co. Ltd., London.

Library of Congress Cataloging in Publication Data
Jones, Robin.
  The art of C programming.
  Includes index.
  1. C (Computer program language) I. Stewart,
Ian. II. Title.
QA76.73.C15J66   1987   005.13'3   86-22014

Typeset by Asco Trade Typesetting Ltd., Hong Kong.
Printed and bound by R.R. Donnelley & Sons, Harrisonburg, Virginia.
Printed in the United States of America.

9 8 7 6 5 4 3 2 1

ISBN 0-387-96392-8 Springer-Verlag New York Berlin Heidelberg
ISBN 3-540-96392-8 Springer-Verlag Berlin Heidelberg New York

"That is my present position," said the Tortoise.

"Then I must ask you to accept C."

"I'll do so," said the Tortoise, "as soon as you've entered it in that notebook of yours."

Lewis Carroll, What the Tortoise Said to Achilles

Preface

The programming language C occupies an unusual position midway between conventional high-level and assembly languages, allowing the programmer to combine the best features of both. This book is an introduction to the language itself, and to the special style of thinking that goes with it. Anyone wishing to learn C is likely to have some experience in a high-level language such as BASIC or Pascal, and it seems sensible to make use of that experience. We therefore assume some facility with conventional notation for computer arithmetic, and simple notions (such as looping and branching) common to most high-level languages.

However, that cannot be the whole story. One cannot learn to speak colloquial French by thinking in English and performing a routine translation. No more can one learn to program in colloquial C by thinking in BASIC and performing a routine translation. However, when learning French it is normal to assume familiarity with English, building on that in the early stages, thereby creating the confidence necessary to provide that *mot juste* to which nothing corresponding exists in English. Our approach to C is similar. In particular we do not introduce at the very beginning some of the features of C which eventually lead to more efficient and elegant code—for example, the ability to do several things, apparently at once. Initially, such constructs can be confusing. Once the reader has acquired some facility with the language it then becomes possible to bring these features into play in a natural manner.

The book divides roughly into two parts. Chapters 1–13 develop the main features of the language itself, accompanied by simple examples, problems (with answers), and—where appropriate—more extensive projects to test the reader's understanding. Chapters 14–17 use these features to develop genuine applications. After all, programs are for *doing* things, and C is fundamentally a systems language. (Indeed C was originally designed in order to write an operating system—namely UNIX—and so is ideally suited for writing general utilities.) We therefore have chosen problems whose solution requires the development of a general utility: rational arithmetic, turtle graphics, and random number generation. Another reason for choosing these topics is that they illustrate different aspects of the language. The rational arithmetic suite makes extensive use of arithmetical bit-manipulation, whereas the random number generator uses logical bit-manipulation. The turtle graphics system requires more sophisticated mathematical ideas. It also shows how to incorporate new facilities into an existing system. An unusual feature of this system is that (in one version) it requires only integer arithmetic.

There are two appendices. The first discusses the remaining topics in the language that are not covered earlier in the book. The second is a quick reference guide. While the book is intended as a tutorial rather than a reference text, this provides a way in which the reader can jog his memory on points of detail.

The approach we have adopted means that in the early chapters some of the code may appear cumbersome. Since we are at that stage deliberately limiting the tools available, this is inevitable. However, by the end of the book the reader will have acquired a relatively thorough grounding in C.

Folkestone, Kent   Robin Jones
Coventry, Warwickshire   Ian Stewart

Contents

CHAPTER 1

Compilers and Interpreters

Alice thought she saw a way out of the difficulty, this time. "If you tell me what language 'fiddle-de-dee' is, I'll tell you the French for it!" she exclaimed triumphantly.

Through the Looking Glass

Any high-level language program must be converted to the native code (or machine language) of the processor on which it ultimately is to run. There are two common approaches to this problem (and a number of less common ones which need not concern us here). The first is to store the program, more or less as it is entered, in the computer's main memory (this is known as *source code*). Then, when the program is executed, to take each line in turn, translate it into machine code and then run the machine code. When the translation of a line takes place, the resulting machine code overwrites that from the previous line, so that if a line of source code appears in a loop which is executed 200 times, it also must be *translated* 200 times. A translator which adopts this strategy is called an *interpreter** and it's the mechanism most familiar to anyone who has used a Commodore 64, Macintosh, IBM PC, or any of the other home micros (or personal computers as the upmarket salesmen prefer to call them).

---

*In practice, modern interpreters are less simple-minded than this, but the principles are broadly the same.

It's obvious that the technique is slow and inefficient, because of the repeated (and therefore unnecessary) translation of lines of code, and because this translation is occurring *while* the program is running. It has, however, one major saving grace. Since, whenever you RUN a program, the interpreter refers to your source code (i.e., the original BASIC program), it is a relatively simple matter to edit and rerun a piece of code—you just revise the BASIC code and type RUN again. (You may be saying to yourself: "What else *could* be necessary?" You'll find out very shortly, and I'm afraid it's a messier process than you're used to.)

The obvious alternative is to translate the entire source code into a single machine code program, and then run the machine code. This will clearly execute faster, and there are no translations during execution. A translator that adopts this approach is called a *compiler*. As a general rule BASIC is interpreted, whereas C is compiled. This isn't to say that you can't have BASIC compilers or C interpreters—both exist—but they are relatively uncommon ways of handling the two languages. Interpreters make ideal development tools because it's so easy to make changes, and that's also why they're useful to beginners; but they aren't good for the professional because of the slow execution of the interpreted code, among other things. Perhaps the ideal software environment would provide you with an interpreter *and* a compiler for identical dialects of the same language. That way, you could use the interpreter until all the debugging was finished, and then compile the final, bug-free program. It goes without saying that Murphy's Law applies, and that therefore where both an interpreter and a compiler exist for a given language on a given machine, there are subtle (and sometimes not so subtle) differences between the dialects of the languages which the two translators deal with. Thus a program which was running happily under the interpreter can suddenly become bug-ridden when it is compiled.

Editors

Somehow you have to create the source program in the first place. A BASIC interpreter has built into it an editor which allows you to type in lines of code, stores them in the right order, enables you to modify them later, and so on. Generally, a compiler has no such utility associated with it, although you may be able to purchase an editor with the compiler. In any event, you must have one before you can get started.

The Compilation Process

The complete ceremony, then, goes something like this:

1. Load the editor.
2. Type in your source program (i.e., the code you want to compile).

3. Save this to backing store.
4. Load the compiler and tell it where to find the source program (in other words, give it the source filename). The compiler will then go through the translation process. There probably will be several passes involved (i.e., the compiler will scan the source more than once). You may have to invoke each pass as a separate program, or the system may handle this for you, depending on how friendly the compiler is. Finally, the compiler will write back to the backing store a machine code version of your source program. However, it won't have included the machine code for any library functions your program uses. So now you must:
5. Load the linker and tell it the name of the machine code file it is to work on. The linker searches this, looking for functions that aren't defined within the file. When it finds one, it looks in the library for it, and links it into the program. Finally it will have created a pure machine code program which it saves to the backing store.
6. At last you have a machine code program that can be loaded from backing store and executed. If the backing store in use is disk, the above process is fairly painless, if somewhat longwinded (I *did* tell you compilers aren't as easy to handle as interpreters). If it is cassette tape you would die of old age before getting anything running. If a compiler designer *expects* this to be the case he may well opt to leave the intermediately generated files in main memory rather than dumping them back to tape, to preserve sanity. The reason this usually isn't done is that allocating a chunk of memory for these files means you can't compile very big programs.

If the foregoing is less than crystal clear at the moment, don't worry. It probably isn't obvious why all these steps are necessary, and it won't be until you've tried a few things out with your C compiler and made some mistakes in the process.

As I've already implied, the *precise* sequence of operations needed will vary from compiler to compiler. Here's a fairly typical one to compile and run a program called FRED.C for the BD Software C compiler running under the CP/M operating system:

System prompt	User response	Effect
A>	CC1 FRED.C	A source file called FRED.C on drive A is passed to the first part of the compiler (CC1). A file called FRED.CCI is created by CC1.
A>	CC2 FRED	The second part of the compiler is invoked on the file FRED.CCI. A file called FRED.CRL is created.
A>	CLINK FRED	The linker is called to insert library functions into FRED.CRL. A file called FRED.COM is created.
A>	FRED	The pure machine code program in the file FRED.COM is loaded and executed.

Actually, in recent versions of this compiler, CC1 automatically chains CC2 provided that no errors have been recognised, so that there is one fewer step necessary. If you're unfamiliar with CP/M, the "$A>$" prompt just indicates that the system is logged on to disk drive A, and it's ready for a further command. Of course, the above sequence assumes no errors have occurred. Errors may be picked up at any stage during the compilation, and appropriate messages will appear on the screen. Whenever one occurs, you must identify the problem and reload the editor to change the source program before repeating the whole process. So changing the odd line is not the trivial process it is in BASIC, and you'll find yourself checking syntax rather more carefully and generally thinking harder about your code because you know that it may take several minutes just to replace a comma with a semicolon, or to change a variable name from I to J.

I'm not trying to dissuade you from using a compiler—the rewards are well worth the extra effort entailed—but you should be aware that you have to pay more attention to detail than is necessary in interpreted BASIC.

Note. You'll have noticed that in this chapter we've consistently referred to ourselves as 'I.' We (I?) have done this because 'we' lacks the informal touch. Henceforth 'we' means 'I and the reader'. If any readers dislike the use of 'I' in a two-author book, they should invoke the flexibility of C and

$$\# \text{ define I we.}$$

(See Chapter 6.)

CHAPTER 2

The Skeleton of a C Program

'Why,' said the Dodo, 'the best way to explain it is to do it.'

Alice's Adventures in Wonderland

Let's now turn our attention to what a C program looks like. All C programs consist of a series of *functions*. A function is somewhat like a BASIC subroutine. The primary difference is that a C function has a built-in mechanism for communicating values to the program which called it (and for accepting values from the calling program).

For example, think about the following BASIC subroutine which evaluates one side of a right angled triangle given the hypotenuse and the other side in the variables *H* and *B*:

```
1000  A = H*H − B*B
1010  If A < 0 THEN PRINT "Invalid triangle": END
1020  X = SQR(A)
1030  RETURN
```

In order to use this, I have to know that the subroutine needs a pair of values to work on, and that these must be placed in two variables called *H* and *B*. Also, I need the information that *X* holds the result. Then I can write something like

$$100 \ H = 7\text{: } B = 3$$
$$110 \ \text{GOSUB } 1000$$
$$120 \ \text{PRINT } X$$

for instance. The subroutine is, in fact, being used as a function because it is being passed values (H and B) and it is returning another (X).

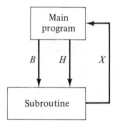

FIGURE 2.1. Communicating between routines.

In the jargon, a function has a set of *arguments* (here H and B) and returns a *value*. However the important point here is that it is the function *itself* which has the returned value, not some variable such as X.

A C function that is equivalent to the subroutine might be

```
tri_side(h, b)
int h, b;
{
        int a, x;
        a = h*h − b*b;
        if (a < 0) {
                printf("Invalid triangle");
                exit(1);
        }
        x = sqr(a);
        return x;
}
```

Plus ca Change ...

As a whole, this won't make much sense yet; but individually, some of the expressions are pretty BASIC-like. For instance

$$a = h*h - b*b;$$

is different only in that it is terminated by a semicolon. Similarly

$$\text{if } (a < 0)$$

isn't a million miles from

$$\text{IF } a < 0 \text{ THEN}$$

and

$$\text{printf(“Invalid triangle”)};$$

is pretty close to

$$\text{PRINT “Invalid triangle”}$$

Vive la Différence

Now for some of the differences. First the function is given a name (tri_side) instead of a starting line number (in fact, there are no line numbers in C). The name may consist of any set of letters (usually lower case, by convention) and the underline symbol is regarded as an honorary letter to improve readability. The number of letters that are significant varies between implementations. Often, it's six, so that the effective name of my function is "tri_si".

The function name is followed by the argument list in brackets, and the arguments are separated by commas.

There are then two statements beginning with the keyword "int", which I want to ignore completely for the time being. There is a "{" symbol between them, however, whose significant I *do* want to deal with.

Simple and Compound Statements

You'll have noticed that every line of the code is terminated by a semicolon. In fact, there may be semicolons *within* a line as well. For instance you could initialize a few variables like this:

$$p = 3; \qquad r = 7; \qquad z = 0;$$

which is just like the BASIC:

$$20 \; P = 3: \qquad R = 7: \qquad Z = 0.$$

The difference is that the semicolons act as statement *terminators* whereas the colons in BASIC act as statement *separators*. A statement in BASIC may be terminated by one other symbol—newline. In C, the newline character has no significance at all. Thus:

$$p = 3;$$

or

$$p =$$
$$3;$$

or

$$p$$
$$=$$
$$3$$
$$;$$

all have the same meaning.

The advantage of this is that groups of statements may run over the end of a line in a way which most BASICs won't allow. How often have you tried to write:

> 2010 IF $a > 7$ OR $b = 3$ OR $c > 0$ THEN (some long sequence of operations that won't fit on a line)

and had to rewrite it as a subroutine when you've realized there's going to be a problem?

On the other hand, if newline doesn't mean anything, how does C know which statements belong in the conditionally executed bit and which don't? Easy! You can combine *simple* statements (those terminated by semicolons) into *compound* statements. A compound statement is a set of simple statements with curly brackets round them. The rule is that if you can put a simple statement somewhere, a compound statement will fit there just as happily. The whole of a C function is a compound statement, so there are curly brackets at its beginning and end. You'll notice that I've lined them up vertically, but that is purely for readability. The compiler doesn't notice spaces, tabs, or newlines, so you can lay out the functions more or less how you like.

You'll see another use of the compound statement idea in the "if" statement:

```
if (a < 0) {
        printf("Invalid triangle");
        exit(1);
}
```

There are two things to do if a is less than zero, so they *have* to be compounded. Incidentally, notice that "if" and all other keywords appear in lower case.

Functions That Don't Return Values

At this stage, I don't want to examine the syntax of the printf function (yes, it *is* a function!) but I do want to look at the next statement:

```
exit(1);
```

This is another function, which will return control to the operating system (somewhat like END in BASIC). exit passes an argument, usually zero if everything has gone smoothly and one if it's an error exit, as here. However, it obviously can't *return* a value. This is quite legitimate. C functions don't have to return anything if it's not appropriate.

Returning Values

Where a function does return a value, we can pass it to a variable as in:

$$x = sqr(a);$$

The value that the function passes back is identified in the return statement:

$$return\ x;$$

Having defined tri_side, then, I can reference it from another function by writing something like:

$$length = tri\_side(hypot, other\_side);$$

This will have the following effects:

1. The contents of hypot are passed to h in tri_side.
2. The contents of other_side are passed to b in tri_side.
3. x is evaluated in tri_side.
4. The contents of x are transferred to length.

Main

If you compare what we have so far with a typical BASIC program, you'll see that there's a rather important element missing—the main program! Since everything in C is a function, it won't surprise you to learn that there must be, in every C program, a function called *main* which acts like the main program in BASIC. This is usually the first function in the program, but it doesn't have to be.

We could write something like this, then:

```
main()
{
        int length, hypot, other_side;
        hypot = 13;
        other_side = 5;
        length = tri_side(hypot, other_side);
        printf("The length is %6d long", length);
}
tri_side(h, b)
int h, b;
{
        int a, x;
        a = h*h − b*b;
        if (a < 0) {
                printf("Invalid triangle");
                exit(1);
```

```
        }
        x = sqr(a);
        return x;
    }
```

main sets up values for hypot and other_side and then calls tri_side, which works out the third side and passes it back, where it's assigned to length. Finally it's printed out (again, don't worry about the printf syntax yet). If a function executes its statements in order and simply falls off the end of the world into its closing curly bracket, no return is necessary (provided, of course, we don't want to return a value), which is why there isn't one at the end of main. Notice also that main takes no arguments, so its brackets are empty. They must be present though.

Immediately below main, tri_side is defined, just as the equivalent BASIC subroutine would have been. There are three further functions:

printf
exit
sqr

The first two will be in the library, so the linker will pick them up, but the chances are that you'd have to write sqr (to evaluate the square root) yourself. We'll examine that problem later.

Variable Types

There remains one keyword that I've used without comment: int. This specifies a variable (or set of variables) to be of *integer* type.

In BASIC, the type of a variable is implied by its name. There are usually only two possibilities. The variable can have no suffix, in which case it's assumed to be able to hold a decimal value (strictly, a floating point number), or it can have a $ suffix in which case it holds a string. Some BASICs allow a % suffix which specifies an integer.

In C, you must declare the type of a variable before you use it. The name itself is not important and the compiler gleans no information from it. We'll come across a number of type specifiers later. For the minute, I'll mention only two:

int
char

The first, as I've already said, indicates integers. The second, fairly obviously, defines characters. So:

    int value, a, zero, fred;
    char c, delim;

declares the variables value, a, zero and fred to be integers, and the variables *c* and delim to be characters. The actual size of an integer is implementation-dependent, but for most micros it's 16 bits, which means that the range of values which can be held is -32768 to 32767. The characters are 1 byte each. So *c* contains *one* character and so does delim. Thus we don't, at the moment, have a way of representing a character *string* at all.

Variable Scope

In BASIC, once you have used a name, a particular chunk of memory is assigned to it, and any subsequent reference to that name is used to relate to that chunk of memory. This is fine most of the time but it does mean that if you reuse a name in a subroutine that you've already assigned in the main program, the new value will overwrite the old one and confuse everybody.

C gets around this problem very simply. A variable defined inside a function has a meaning only *inside* that function. We say that the *scope* of the variable is limited to the function. For instance, in our example program, *a* and *x* are meaningless outside tri_side. Similarly, hypot has a meaning only inside main because that's where it's defined.

This is why we *need* a mechanism (the parameter list and the return statement) for transferring data between functions; as soon as a function is left the values stored in its variables are lost. It also means that we don't have to worry about reusing names; a variable *y* in main would be quite distinct from a variable *y* in tri_side.

You'll notice that I've also made a distinction between parameters that are *passed* to a function and those that are local to it. In tri_side, I've written:

```
tri_side(h, b)
int h, b;
{
        int a, x;
```

when you might have expected:

```
{
        int h, b, a, x;
```

This is true because C expects to see arguments defined *immediately* after they're referenced. Otherwise, it will assume them to be integers. If it then finds a type specification within the body of the function it will claim that this is a redeclaration, not unnaturally. So type declarations for function arguments must appear before the function body, as I've shown.

Global Variables

Of course, there may be circumstances in which we actually *want* all the functions in a program to have access to a particular variable. Such a variable is called *global*, and it must be defined outside all functions, including main.

Thus a program might appear as:

```
int a;
main()
{
        int b;
        :
        a = a + b;
        :
}
function(b, c)
int b, c;
{

        :
        a = a + c;
        :

}
```

The variable "a" now has exactly the same meaning within *main* and *function*, so "b" and "c" are being added into the same cell.

Loose Ends

I have (deliberately) been less than precise in this chapter, and I've committed a number of sins of omission. For instance the scope rules I've just outlined are very incomplete. My defence is that at this stage, I'm simply trying to give you an idea of the general appearance of a piece of C code, without getting too involved in detail. In later chapters I shall return to all of the points so far touched on.

For example, the statements

```
x = sqr(a);
return x;
```

could be replaced by

```
return sqr(a);
```

and similarly

```
length = tri_side(hypot, other_side);
printf("The length is %6d long", length);
```

is the same as

```
printf("The length is %6d long", tri_side(hypot, other_side));
```

Whether this kind of code compaction is desirable is a matter of opinion. It can lead to *very* obscure code.

printf

I have, up to now, avoided explaining the syntax of the printf (for "print formatted") function. I'll give a brief introduction to it here, although, again, there is more to come later. The first argument is a string, enclosed in double quotes, which is printed out as it stands *unless* it contains a "%" symbol. So for instance

printf("This is a message");

will print out

This is a message

However,

printf("The length is %4d cms", 1);

will print:

The length is ———— cms

and the characters I've marked with minus signs will contain the value of 1. Thus the "%4d" says "insert in the next 4 character spaces the value in decimal (hence the *d*) of the next argument" (in this case 1). Similarly:

printf("1st value: %3d; 2nd value: %5d", x, y);

would print:

1st value: ———;   2nd value: —————

with the value in x occupying the first 3 blanks and the value in y appearing in the next 5.

Comments

I have not included any comments in the sample functions introduced in this chapter. C does allow for them (just as BASIC does with REM). They can appear almost anywhere, between the symbol pairs /∗ and ∗/.

For example, if I wanted to remind myself that the sqr function does not yet exist, I could terminate the appropriate line of code like this:

$x = $ sqr(a); /∗ Not yet written !! ∗/

It is, of course, good practice to comment your code, but you will see very few lines of commented code in this book. That is true because most of the functions outlined are the subject of detailed description in the text, so that to add comments in the listings would be superfluous. To be useful, comments must illuminate the code. Unhelpful comments appear too often. For instance, I have seen the following line, written by a professional programmer:

$$i = 0; /* \text{ set i to zero } */$$

Honest!

These are simple warm-up exercises to let you flex your C muscles. If you need a function that is standard in BASIC, such as SQR, you may assume that the corresponding C function sqr() exists.

1. Write a C function that returns the area of a triangle whose sides are a, b, c. Use the formula

$$A = \sqrt{s(s - a)(s - b)(s - c)}$$

where $s = \frac{1}{2}(a + b + c)$. Your program should check that it is possible to form a triangle with the given sides, and print the message "impossible triangle" if not.

2. What does the following function do?

```
conv(t)
{
    int t, u;
    u = 5*(t − 32)/9;
    return u;
}
```

3. Write a function *vnoc* that undoes what *conv* does.

4. Write a program to find the prime factors of an integer.

5. Light travels at 186,000 miles per second. An astronomical unit is 93 million miles. Write a function delay(d) that returns the time that it takes a radio message to reach a space probe at a distance of d astronomical units from the transmitter.

CHAPTER 3

Loops and Control Constructs

"Then you keep moving around, I suppose?" said Alice.
"Exactly so," said the Hatter: "as the things get used up."
"But what happens when you come to the beginning again?" Alice
ventured to ask.

Alice's Adventures in Wonderland

All modern computer languages provide a number of control structures
that allow you to execute a piece of code once or repeatedly as long as
some condition is true. In BASIC we have IF..THEN (and sometimes
IF..THEN..ELSE) and FOR..NEXT.

C has a rather more powerful range of such constructs.

If

Let's deal with "if" first of all, since we've already met it in passing. Its general
form is:

> if (condition)
>> statement1
>
> else
>> statement2

statement1 and statement2 can, of course, be simple or compound statements
and the else clause is optional. The conditional operators are a little unusual.

Where, in BASIC, you might write:

$$\text{IF } a = 7 \text{ THEN}\ldots$$

in C you would write:

$$\text{if } (a == 7)\ldots$$

The double equals sign is *very* important. If you don't put it in the effect is *not* to generate a syntax error, but to do something unexpected. The results can be very confusing. The reason for it is that C needs to be able to distinguish between an assignment and an equality. For instance:

$$a = 7;$$

means "put 7 into *a*", whereas:

$$a == 7$$

means "compare *a* with 7". (Actually that isn't *quite* true; see the next section.) BASIC lives with the ambiguity of using the equals symbol to mean two different things. But C, like most other modern languages, refuses to compromise here, which makes life easier for the compiler and, as we shall see later, allows for some more powerful constructs.

Conditional Expressions

Now to clear up a little terminological inexactitude (as Richard Nixon's press secretary used to say) that I've just perpetrated.

C *evaluates* a conditional expression (such as $x > 3$ or $a == 7$) to 1 or 0 depending on whether it is true or false. Thus the value of $x > 3$ is 1 if $x = 5$, 0 if $x = 3$. However, statement1 will be executed for *any* non-zero value of the conditional expression in the brackets. So you can write

$$\text{if } (x > 0) \text{ printf}(\text{"}x \text{ is positive"});$$

which is what you'd expect, but also

$$\text{if } (x) \text{ printf}(\text{"}x \text{ is not zero"});$$

(Notice that there's no need for curly brackets here because only a simple statement follows the condition.)

You can negate a conditional expression by preceding it with an exclamation mark. Thus

$$\text{if } (x == 0) \text{ printf}(\text{"}x \text{ is zero"});$$

is exactly equivalent to

$$\text{if } (!x) \text{ printf}(\text{"}x \text{ is zero"});$$

The exclamation mark can also precede a conditional operator to negate its effect. The complete set of conditional operators is:

== is equal to	!= is not equal to
> is greater than	< is less than
>= is greater than or equal to	<= is less than or equal to

Notice that one of the equals symbols is *replaced* by the exclamation mark in "is not equal to", and that the order of the symbols in ">=" and "<=" *is* significant. If you write them the other way round, you'll almost certainly confuse the compiler.

Logical Connectives

Combinations of conditional expressions can be formed using the connectives && (and) and || (or). This leads to statements like:

$$\text{if } (a > 10 \text{ \&\& } a < 20)$$
$$\text{printf("a is within range");}$$

The whole expression could be negated:

$$\text{if } (!(a > 10 \text{ \&\& } a < 20))$$
$$\text{printf("a is not within range");}$$

Notice the use of brackets here to make the "not" apply to the whole expression. The precedence of the && and || operators is not always defined the same way by different compilers so it's sensible to use brackets wherever they are used together to make your meaning totally clear. For example

$$\text{if } ((x >= 10 \text{ \&\& } x <= 50) || y == 0)$$

means

$$\text{if } x \text{ lies in the range 10 to 50 or } y \text{ is zero}$$

whereas

$$\text{if } (x >= 10 \text{ \&\& } (x <= 50 || y == 0))$$

requires the value of x to be at least 10 *regardless* of the value of y.

Loops

There are a number of ways of forming loops in C. All use the conditional expression concept that we've already seen in the "if" statement.

while

This is the simplest loop format. Its general form is

$$\text{while (condition)}$$
$$\text{statement}$$

As long as the condition is true (i.e., non-zero), the statement (which, as usual, may be simple or compound) will be executed.

Let's take a simple example. We'll write a program to evaluate the cubes of integers between 1 and 20. It looks like this:

```
main()
{
    int value, cube;
    value = 1;
    while (value < 21) {
        cube = value*value*value;
        printf("%2d   %5d", value, cube);
        value = value + 1;
    }
}
```

Let's take this statement by statement. First, value and cube are declared to be variables of type integer. Next value is initialized to 1. Now the loop is entered, and its contents will be executed, since value *is* less than 21. (If value *were* to be 21 on entry, the loop would never be executed at all. Compare this with the action of a FOR-NEXT loop which will always execute once regardless of the initial conditions.) The cube is evaluated, value and cube are printed out, and value is incremented by 1. Since that's the end of the loop, the test is made again, and the whole thing will be repeated until value reaches 21. That's a neat structure isn't it? It gets better....

Autoincrements

In most languages, there is a need to increment variables pretty frequently. We've just seen it in:

$$value = value + 1;$$

which is (give or take a semicolon) identical to its BASIC equivalent. But C recognises the popularity of this kind of structure and provides a special form for it. This is:

$$value++;$$

which you can read as "increment value by 1". Now the significance of this isn't just that it's slightly quicker to write "$f++$;" rather than "$f = f + 1$;", say. It is, rather, that the compiler can now distinguish between an increment and a common or garden addition, and handle them differently. It can't tell the difference between "$f = f + 1$;" and "$a = b + c$;". In the latter case it has to find where b is, find where c is, add them together, find where a is and place the result there. It will treat "$f = f + 1$;" much the same way. But "$f++$" is a different kettle of fish. The compiler *knows* it's just an increment and will implement it as a single *machine code* increment instruction, which means it only references *f* once.

This kind of philosophy makes C compilers relatively efficient (i.e., they produce machine code which isn't too much more convoluted than might be written by a human programmer), so the final machine code program can be fairly small and will execute very fast.

There's more. You can increment a variable *whenever* you mention it in any context. So I could rewrite the cubes program like this:

```
main()
{
    int value, cube;
    value = 0;
    while (value++ < 20) {
        cube = value*value*value;
        printf("%2d   %5d", value, cube);
    }
}
```

Now value is incremented immediately *after* the test is made. Consequently, I've initialized it to 0. Otherwise, it would be 2 on entering the loop for the first time. Because the increment occurs after the test, I've also had to change the boundary value to 20. I could have made the increment occur *before* the test by writing:

$$++value$$

in which case the boundary changes back to 21.

There is one final simplification which is possible:

```
main()
{
    int value;
    value = 0;
    while (value++ < 20)
        printf("%2d   %5d", value, value*value*value);
}
```

Now one of the arguments of printf *is* the calculation, so there's only a simple statement in the while loop. Consequently we lose a pair of curly brackets.

Incidentally, decrements can be performed in an equivalent way to increments, for example by using things like *x*−−.

The sqr Function

In Chapter 2, I made use of a square root function (which I called sqr) and then blithely remarked that it probably wasn't present in your compiler's library. Never mind; let's write it now.

There's a simple relationship which states that if you're trying to take the square root of n, and you have an approximation x to it, then a better approximation is:

$$(x^2 + n)/(2x).$$

It doesn't matter how bad your initial approximation is, this formula will produce a better one. So you can use the better one to generate a better one still, and so on, until you get as close as you like to the right answer.

Here's a first attempt at the function, using this idea:

```
sqr(n)
int n;
{
        int approx;
        approx = 1;
        while (n != approx*approx)
                approx = (approx*approx + n)/(2*approx);
        return approx;
}
```

This is straightforward enough. The approximation is initialised to 1. While the current approximation squared isn't equal to n (the value being square rooted), the formula is evaluated and the result put back into approx. As soon as they *are* the same, the loop is exited and the current value of approx is returned.

However, bear in mind that I've declared everything as integers. My main reason for doing this is that on some common C compilers, it's the only numeric data type implemented. If you are mucking about with square roots for real, you obviously need to be able to handle numbers that include decimal fractions. C calls this type *float* (for floating point). For the time being, we're going to do without it.

It is instructive to examine the precise effect of the function on a couple of values. First, let's try 16. The initial value of approx is 1, so the next value will be $(1*1 + 16)/(2*1) = 17/2 = 8$. It should be 8.5, of course, but it will actually be truncated because it is an integer. Then you'll get $(8*8 + 16)/(2*8) = 80/16 = 5$. The next value is $41/10 = 4$, and that will satisfy the while condition, so the loop is exited and 4 is returned, correctly.

However, if you repeat the trick with $n = 21$, you'll get the sequence 11, 6, 4, 4, 4, ..., going around the loop forever.

In other words, the algorithm converges on 4 (as it should, because this is the nearest integer *below* the square root of 21), but the while condition is never satisfied because 4*4 isn't 21! This problem is certainly emphasised by my insistence on sticking to integers, but it would *still* be present if you used floating point variables. To any given degree of precision, there are infinitely many numbers whose square roots cannot be represented exactly. So it's unrealistic to *expect* the condition $n ==$ approx*approx to be met at all!

Obviously, we need to build in a maximum allowable error. One way of approaching the problem would be to see whether *n* is contained between the squares of approx and approx + 1:

while (!(*n* > aprox∗approx && *n* < (approx + 1)∗(approx + 1)))...

but that looks a bit messy. Alternatively, we could use the way the sequence *converges*, by comparing two successive values of approx. If their difference is less than our required error limit we exit the loop. This leads to the following revision:

```
sqr(n)
int n;
{
     int approx, new_approx;
     approx = 1; new_approx = 0;
     while (approx − new_approx >= 1) {
          new_approx = (approx∗approx + n) / (2∗approx);
          approx = new_approx;
     }
     return new_approx;
}
```

Wait a bit though, that isn't quite right! We keep a temporary reference to the old approximation O.K., but we destroy it with the last statement in the loop, so that, second time round, approx and new_approx are guaranteed to be the same!

How about this, then?

```
sqr(n)
int n;
{
     int approx, new_approx, forever;
     approx = 1; forever = 1;
     while (forever) {
          new_approx = (approx∗approx + n) / (2∗approx);
          if (approx − new_approx < 1)
               return new_approx;
          approx = new_approx;
     }
}
```

Now the loop is executed indefinitely so far as the while condition is concerned, because forever is set to 1 (i.e., true). I could have written:

while (1)

but the meaning is less clear. Inside the loop, the if statement decides whether to continue the loop or return from the function.

Problem 1

There is still a bug here. Usually approx is greater than new_approx so we
have, in calculating the square root of 21, for example,

$$11 - 6 = 5 : \text{not less than 1 so don't return}$$
$$6 - 4 = 2 : \text{not less than 1 so don't return}$$
$$4 - 4 = 0 : \text{less than 1; return}$$

However, on the *first* time through the loop approx = 1, so the if condition
gives $1 - 11 = -10$ which *is* less than 1. Oops!

You could get around this by mimicking BASIC's ABS function which
simply strips off any minus sign present:

    if (abs(approx − new_approx) < 1)
            return new_approx;

Write a C abs function.

It may seem that it is possible to use a while loop for almost any purpose,
and that other looping structures are unnecessary. At one level, that is true,
but there are times when alternative arrangements are more convenient. C
provides two other structures. The first is ...

do − while

This has the form:

                do
                        statement
                while (condition);

It is, fairly obviously, an upside down while loop because the conditional
expression is evaluated *after* the statement has been executed. So the statement
is obeyed at least once regardless of the truth or falsity of the condition.

This gives us another way to handle the sqr function:

```
sqr(n)
int n;
{
     int approx, new_approx;
     new approx = 1;
     do {
          approx = new_approx;
          new_approx = (approx*approx + n) / (2*approx);
     } while (abs(approx − new_approx) >= 1);
     return new_approx;
}
```

Now, the original problem with while has gone away, because the test is made
before the values in approx and new_approx have been equated. On the other

hand, an unnecessary transfer takes place on the first loop, which requires us to give new_approx a dummy value (it doesn't matter what—I've chosen 1 at random). Some compilers would be happy if you don't do this, but it's bad practice not to be *sure* what's happening in a program.

Problem 2

Rewrite the cubes program using a do–while loop.

for loops

Finally, there's the good old for loop, which doesn't look *too* unlike its BASIC forbear. Here's an example:

$$\text{for } (n = 1; n < 50; n++) \{$$
$$\cdots\cdots$$
$$\cdots\cdots$$
$$\}$$

The meaning is pretty clear. The first expression ($n = 1$) identifies the starting value for n, the second ($n < 50$) gives the condition for which the loop will continue to be executed, and the third gives the incremental details. So the above statement is equivalent to the BASIC:

$$\text{FOR } N = 1 \text{ TO } 49 \text{ STEP } 1$$

except that, as with while, the test occurs at the top of the loop, and of course the BASIC version doesn't actually *need* the "STEP 1", whereas the "$n++$" is obligatory in C.

What happens, though, if you want an increment other than 1? The third expression can be a simple statement, so that:

$$\text{for}(n = 1; n <= 50; n = n + 5)$$

would be equivalent to:

$$\text{FOR } N = 1 \text{ TO } 50 \text{ STEP } 5$$

There is a more convenient form of $n = n + 5$, however. It is:

$$n += 5;$$

This has the same advantage in terms of compilation efficiency as the auto-increment form; n is only referenced once. It can be used with any arithmetic operator. So:

$$y *= 51 \quad \text{means "multiply } y \text{ by 51"}$$
$$a -= 2 \quad \text{means "decrement } a \text{ by 2"}$$

and

$$r /= 3 \quad \text{means "divide } r \text{ by 3"}$$

The C for loop is much more flexible than its BASIC stablemate. For instance, there is nothing at all to stop me writing:

$$\text{for}(n = 5; i != 60; p \mathbin{*}= 3)$$

in which case n is initialised to 5, the loop is executed only as long as i isn't 60, and p is multiplied by 3 after every pass through it.

Problem 3

You'll have noticed that whenever I've wanted to take a power of a number, I've used successive multiplication. This is so because there is no power operator in C. The "$\wedge$" symbol, which BASIC uses for this purpose, exists, but it has another meaning. Write a function:

$$\text{power(number, } n)$$

which returns number to the power n, using a for loop.

Answers

Problem 1

One solution is:

```
abs(value)
int value;
{
        if (value < 0)
                value = -value;
        return value;

}
```

There are other possibilities, like writing

$$\text{value} \mathbin{*}= -1;$$

instead of

$$\text{value} = -\text{value};$$

but there is usually a good case to be made for making code as clear as possible.

Problem 2

```
main()
{
    int value;
    value = 1;
    do
            printf("%2d   %5d", value, value*value*value);
        while (value++ < 20);

}
```

There is nothing much to comment on here, except to clarify a point that may have been worrying you. Since value can be incremented anywhere, why do so in the while condition rather than inside the printf argument list? This is possible, but it's *very* bad form, because the order in which such increments occur inside a function call is not defined. Consequently the effect will vary between compilers, whereas your object should be to write portable code.

Problem 3

```
power(number, n)
int number, n;
{
        int count, result;
        result = 1;
        for (count = 1; count <= n; count++)
            result *= number;
        return result;

}
```

This will, of course, only work for positive numbers, but it does handle $n = 0$ correctly, because the loop is never executed, count being immediately greater than n, and so 1 is returned.

PROJECTS

1. Write a C program to print-out a complete set of multiplication tables for numbers from 1 to 12:
   (a) Using for loops,
   (b) Using while loops,
   (c) Using do/while loops.

2. If x is an approximation to the cube root of n, then

$$(2x^3 + n)/3x^2$$

   is a better one. Use this fact to write a function cbrt(n) which evaluates the cube root of n.

3. In arithmetic modulo n numbers are replaced by their remainder on division by n. (For example 15 modulo 7 is 1 because $15 = 2*7 + 1$.) Write a program to print out addition and multiplication tables for the numbers $0, 1, \ldots, n - 1$ modulo n, for $n = 1, \ldots, 10$.

CHAPTER 4

Arithmetic and Logic

...and then the different branches of arithmetic—Ambition, Distraction,
Uglification, and Derision

Alice's Adventures in Wonderland

"Contrariwise," continued Tweedledee, "if it ain't so, it might be, and if
it were so, it would be; but as it isn't, it ain't. That's logic."

Through the Looking Glass

It seems a little late to introduce arithmetic now, when we've been using it with wild abandon for the last two chapters. Up to now, though, all the symbols I have used have had the same meanings in BASIC, except for the increment and decrement operators, which I introduced separately. So far then, we have:

+	add
−	subtract
*	multiply
/	divide
++	increment by 1
−−	decrement by 1

There is one more to deal with: the modulus operator (%). This gives the *remainder* of a division. For example:

8 % 3 = 2, the remainder when 8 is divided by 3.

As we shall see in Chapter 15, there is a subtle distinction between this and a *true* mathematical mod operation. For the time being, we'll ignore it.

Odds and Evens

An obvious use of this is to determine whether a value is odd or even. Let's write a function called even which returns 1 if its argument is even and 0 if it's odd.

```
even(n)
int n;
{
        if (n % 2)
                return 0;
        else
                return 1;
}
```

That needs a little thought; if n is odd, dividing it by 2 will leave a remainder, so n % 2 will be true. Hence 0 should be returned. If it's even, n % 2 is false (0) so we return 1.

Now, in some other function, I can write:

```
if (even(number))
        printf("%4d is even", number);
```

for example. As you see, this reads pretty nicely, and its function is immediately apparent. It is a matter of good programming style that this should be so.

Logical Operators

Anyone who has played around with machine code will be familiar with the logical operations AND, OR, NOT and XOR. Anyone who hasn't probably won't be. There's a good reason for that. Most high level languages certainly don't encourage you to use them and some positively prohibit their use. This is a pity because, in some circumstances, they provide a set of powerful tools for problem solving. C gives you direct access to the lot. I'll assume you haven't met them and deal with each one in detail. If you are familiar with the techniques you'll be able to skim through this, although, of course, the C syntax will be new.

I'm going to hang most of the examples which follow on to the general area of character-handling techniques, so all variables will be declared to be of type char. I'll assume that a "char" is an eight-bit byte, which is a pretty safe bet, regardless of your machine or compiler.

ASCII Code

You'll probably be familiar with the numerical coding of characters because BASIC gives you access to its thinking on the subject via the ASC function. You probably even remember some of the more common values: "A" = 65, "1" = 49 for instance. If you think about the ASCII coding system in binary, though, it's possible to see what information is contributed by each *bit*:

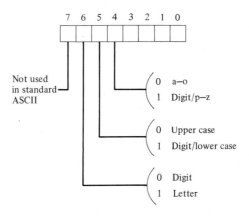

So, for example, if bit 6 is 1 (and therefore the symbol is a letter), bit 5 determines whether it is upper or lower case. I have, for the purpose in hand, completely ignored special symbols such as ∗ ? ! etc. and control characters.

AND

The AND operation compares two bit patterns and produces a third result pattern. If corresponding pairs of bits are both '1' the result bit for that position is set to '1'. Under all other circumstances it is set to '0'.

For instance, suppose there are two bytes p and q with the bit patterns shown below:

$$p \quad\quad 01101001$$
$$q \quad\quad 10111010$$

Then:

$$p \mathbin{\&} q = 00101000$$

[i.e., if p AND q contain 1's in a given column, the result bit is 1]. I've used the C notation for AND (&). You'll remember the logical connective &&

which also means 'and', but in the context of a conditional expression. The single ampersand symbol represents a 'bitwise AND'.

Now to use this idea on our ASCII characters. Suppose that we have a character entered but we don't check on its case on input. For convenience, we would like to standardize on upper case. So we need a function called toupper that will leave upper case letters alone, but convert lower case to their upper case equivalents. Here it is:

```
toupper(c)
char c;
{
        char mask;
        mask = 223;
        return (c & mask);
}
```

That's breathtakingly simple. How does it work? Well, think about the binary value of 223:

$$11011111$$

AND this with any pattern

abcdefgh

and what you get is

ab0defgh

So bit 5 is forced to zero, and the other bits are left unchanged; exactly what we need for an upper case letter, assuming, as I said before, that we are sure c *was* a letter in the first place.

Notice that, although I declared mask to be a char, C is quite happy to pass a number to it (in mask = 223;). The language will allow most (sensible) type conversions of this kind. The term "mask" is commonly used in this kind of context. It's very descriptive. Bit 5 is, indeed, hidden or masked out.

In fact I didn't really need the extra variable at all. I could have written

return (c & 223);

Problem 1

Write a function same_start(p, q) which returns 1 if bytes p, q start with the same bit, and zero if they start with different bits.

OR

Like AND, OR compares two bit patterns and generates a resulting pattern. If either of the corresponding pairs of bits is a '1' the result bit for that column is '1'. Only if both bits are zero is the result zero. For instance:

$$p \quad 01101010$$
$$q \quad 00100011$$
$$p \mid q \text{ is} \quad 01101011$$

[i.e., if p OR q contains a '1' in a given column the result bit is 1].

The symbol for bitwise OR is a single vertical bar, which is consistent with the logical connective equivalent.

This operator allows us to write the tolower function, which will form lower case letters from either upper or lower case arguments:

```
tolower (c)
char c;
{
        char mask;
        mask = 32;
        return (c | mask);
}
```

This time the mask pattern is:

$$00100000$$

OR this with:

abcdefgh

and the result is:

ab1defgh

and you can see that bit 5 is forced to 1, giving a lower case letter. Actually, more sophisticated versions of toupper and tolower probably will be in your compiler's library, but the next one may not be.

Problem 2

Write a function same_ends(p) that returns 1 if a byte p starts and ends with the same bit, and 0 if not.

XOR

This is short for eXclusive OR. It's like OR except that it *excludes* the condition that both bits are '1'.

So, to take the same example as for OR:

$$p \quad 01101010$$
$$q \quad 00100011$$
$$p \wedge q \text{ is} \quad 01001001$$
$$1 \wedge 1 = 0.$$

The C symbol for XOR is $\wedge$.

Now we can write the function swapcase, which converts lower to upper case and vice versa.

```
swapcase(c)
char c;
{
        char mask;
        mask = 32;
        return (c ∧ mask);
}
```

Consider the effect of this on our general pattern:

abcdefgh
00100000
ab?defgh

'*a*' will be reproduced in the result pattern whatever it is, because $1 \wedge 0 = 1$ and $0 \wedge 0 = 0$. Obviously the same goes for *b*, *d*, *e*, *f*, *g* and *h*. Now look at '*c*'.

If $c = 0$ we have $0 \wedge 1 = 1$
If $c = 1$ we have $1 \wedge 1 = 0$

So bit '*c*' is switched (or *toggled*) between 0 and 1, thus swapping the case over.

NOT

There's one remaining logical operator, NOT. This inverts every bit in a field. For instance:

p   01110001
~ *p*   10001110

You'll see that the NOT operator symbol is a tilde (~).

Here's one possible use for it. Imagine that you're writing a traffic simulation program that involves traffic lights. So you could have the definitions:

```
char red, green, light;
red = 0; green = 255;
```

for instance. (255 sets all bits of the byte to 1.) Now you can write statements like:

```
if(light == red)....
```

You could also write an extremely simple function to change the light:

```
change (light)
char light;
{
        return (~light);
}
```

Problem 3

I began this discussion by remarking that an 8-bit byte was pretty much a racing certainty. However, there do exist a (relatively) few machines with a 9-bit byte, 6 bits used to be a fairly common standard and who is to say that machines with 10-bit bytes may not become all the rage?

Clearly, at least some of the code I have been presenting fails to work if confronted with one of these newfangled machines.

The trick is to write code which does not depend for its correct functioning on such unknowns. Can you rewrite the traffic light code snippet in such a way that it is implementation independent?

Shifts

If you shift a bit pattern left and fill in to the right with zeros it has the effect of multiplying by 2. For instance:

$$p : 00010011 = 19$$
$$\text{shift left one bit} : 00100110 = 38$$
$$\uparrow$$
$$\text{fill with a zero}$$

This can be done directly in C:

$$y = x << 1;$$

will shift x left 1 bit and put the result in y. Similarly:

$$p = r << 4;$$

would shift r 4 bits left, resulting in a multiplication by 16.

These operations are *much* faster than performing conventional multiplications, particularly on cheap microcomputers that have no hardware multiply. So they can be very useful in time-critical routines. Here's a "multiply by ten" using this technique:

```
times10(n)
int n;
{
        int m, p;
        m = n << 1;
        p = m << 2;
        return (m + p);
}
```

First n is shifted left 1 bit, so $m = 2n$. Then p is evaluated as $4m$ which is $8n$. So the returned value is $2n + 8n = 10n$.

Right shifts are also possible:

$$a = b >> 2;$$

would shift b 2 bits right and put the result in a. (Incidentally, if you want the result in b you could write $b >>= 2$, just as you can write $b += 2$.)

Normally, a right shift is equivalent to a divide by 2, as you'd expect, but there are exceptions to this rule which we'll come across later.

Problem 4

Write a function agree(p, q) which returns 1 if the top 3 bits of p are the same as the bottom 3 bits of q, *or* the top 3 bits of q are the same as the bottom 3 bits of p.

p ∗∗∗.. +++

                      at least one pair agrees.

q +++ .. ∗∗∗

Answers

Problem 1

```
same_start(p, q)
char p, q;
{
    char mask;
    mask = 128;
    return (p & mask == q & mask);
}
```
OR:
```
same_start(p, q)
char p, q;
{
    return (p & 128 == q & 128);
}
```

Problem 2

```
same_ends(p)
char p;
{
    return ((p & 129 == 0) | (p & 129 == 129));
}
```

Explanation: $129 = 10000001$. So if $p = abcdefgh$, then p & $129 = a000000h$. If $a = h$ this is 00000000 OR 10000001.

Problem 3

It's deceptively simple; just write:

red = 0;   green = ˜red;

Thus red sets all bits of the byte to zero regardless of its size, and green is set up to invert all of them.

Problem 4

I'll do this via a second function $ag(p, q)$ which does *half* the job:

```
agree(p, q)
char p, q;
{
      return (ag(p, q) | ag(q, p));
}
ag(p, q)
char p, q;
{
      return (((p & 224) >> 5) == (q & 7));
}
```

Note that $11100000 = 224, 00000111 = 7$.

CHAPTER 5

Strings, Arrays, and Pointers

They had a large canvas bag, which tied at the mouth with strings: into this they slipped the guinea-pig, head first, and then sat upon it.

Alice's Adventures in Wonderland

Thus far in our discussions, there have been two glaring omissions: any reference to string handling and any reference to arrays. In most BASICs, a string is held in an array, but the connection is not made explicit. In C, the relationship between strings and arrays is much more evident, so we can kill two birds with one stone.

Strings and Pointers

We have already met strings briefly, as arguments in a printf function

printf("This is a string");

for example. It appears that there is nothing very unusual here—a string is enclosed in double quote marks, just like its BASIC equivalent. So I ought to be able to write

$$s = \text{"this message"};$$

and then, later

$$\text{printf}(s);$$

Again, just like BASIC. Indeed I *can* do these things (although, for reasons which will become apparent shortly, it's very inadvisable), and this fact is *totally* misleading because it masks the method C uses for thinking about strings. So what's *really* going on?

When C compiles a statement like

$$s = \text{"this message"};$$

it sets up a set of consecutive bytes somewhere in memory:

38012	t
38013	h
38014	i
38015	s
38016	
38017	m
38018	e
38019	s
38020	s
38021	a
38022	g
38023	e
38024	0 [ASCII null delimiter]

I've shown a set of possible actual addresses which might be used. There's nothing special, of course, about 38012, but subsequent bytes follow the obvious sequence through memory. You'll notice that there's a delimiter provided by the system, which is a zero byte. That's *not* ASCII zero (whose value is 48) but ASCII null (i.e., all bits set to '0').

Now for the unusual bit. The variable s is set to 38012. In other words, it is *not* the string but rather a *pointer* to the string. The idea of a pointer is central to the C programming philosophy and I shall have a lot more to say about it later. For the moment it is enough to note that it is pointers to strings, rather than the strings themselves, that are passed around in a C program. Even in the "print a message" case

$$\text{printf}(\text{"some output"});$$

the argument that is really passed to printf is the pointer to the string "some output."

Arrays

As we shall see, there are significant advantages to be gained from the notion of using a pointer to a string, rather than the string itself. However, I first want to focus on an apparent disadvantage.

In BASIC, I could have written

$$a\$ = \text{``this message''}$$

and then later

$$a\$ = a\$ + \text{``something else''}$$

In C, an attempt to do this same kind of operation (i.e., to put 's' in 38024, 'o' in 38025, 'm' in 38026, etc.) would be almost certainly doomed to disaster. The trouble is that any storage allocated chronologically after the original string will also follow it physically, so it's a Cray X-MP to an IBM PC that this memory is already occupied by useful information. C will be quite happy to allow you to overwrite it, and will take no responsibility for the result, which probably will be a baffling crash.

Declaring Arrays

The solution is fairly obvious: set up an array that can hold any desired string comfortably. An array can be declared in a type declaration statement. For example

$$\text{char } s[30];$$

sets up an array of 30 bytes. Similarly

$$\text{int } n[150];$$

declares an array of 150 integers. Obviously this is pretty similar to BASIC's DIM statement, but there are some differences. First, square brackets are used for array subscripts. Second, the range of subscripts set up for s is 0–29, and that for n is 0–149. In other words, the value in the brackets identifies the *number* of elements in the array, not, as it would in BASIC, the highest subscript.

We're still left with the problem of getting the characters into the array in the first place. We'll assume there's a function called strcpy which will do the job (I'll describe it in detail later). So I can write

$$\text{strcpy}(s, \text{``some stuff''});$$

to transfer the string "some stuff" to the array s. There's an important implication here. If I were to expand the above statement

$$p = \text{``some stuff''};$$
$$\text{strcpy}(s, p);$$

it becomes evident that p and s are the same sort of animal. They are *both* pointers! So: *An array name is a pointer to the beginning of the array.* However, there is one difference: an array name is a constant and you can't do arithmetic with it (although I know of one C compiler that allows this!) whereas a pointer can be manipulated in any way you like.

String Functions

Let's illustrate these ideas by writing functions that mimic BASIC's LEN, LEFT$, RIGHT$, and MID$.

So first we want a function that is passed a pointer to the string, and will return the number of bytes the string contains:

```
len(s)
char s[];
{
        int k;
        k = 0;
        while (s[k++])
            ;
        return (k − 1);
}
```

This needs some explanation. First notice that we need to tell C that s is an array of type char, but we don't have to tell it how big s is. This is a good thing, because when the function is written, we don't know the size of s, but in many languages we would have to declare s to be bigger than anything that's likely to come along, thus wasting memory. As you see, we leave our options open simply by not entering a value between the square brackets. C sorts the problem out by allocating space to s only when it knows how much the calling functions needs (or at least, that's how the mechanism appears; can you deduce what really happens?).

Now for the body of the function. The basic algorithm is reasonably obvious. We look through the array searching for an ASCII null and counting as we go. The count and array subscript are (virtually) the same thing so I've used just one variable (k) for both. Initially, k is zero, so we examine $s[k]$. But we know that this will need to be incremented so why not write $s[k++]$? Now we want to keep executing the loop until we find a zero. I could have written:

$$\text{while } (s[k++] \mathrel{!=} 0)$$

but that has exactly the same meaning as "while $s[k++]$ is true" which is

$$\text{while } (s[k++]).$$

What is it that we need to do inside the loop? Just increment 1; but that's already done! So the loop is empty and just requires a terminating semicolon.

Finally notice that $k − 1$ is returned. To confirm that this is correct, think about the most trivial possible example—the null string. As soon as $s[k]$ is tested it is incremented, so it will be 1 on leaving the loop, which is one too many.

The Left-Hand Bit

For reasons that I'll temporarily defer, it isn't very convenient to produce a direct equivalent of BASIC's

$$b\$ = \text{LEFT\$}(a\$,6)$$

or whatever. It's better to make the original string *and* its substring arguments of the function, so that the equivalent C function call would be

$$\text{left } (a, b, 6);$$

where a and b are pointers to strings and b will end up pointing to the leftmost 6 characters pointed to by a.

Here's one solution:

```
left(string, sub, n)
char string[], sub[];
int n;
{
    int i;
    for (i = 0;     i < n;     i++)
        sub[i] = string[i];
    sub[i] = 0;
}
```

There's nothing really new here. n bytes are copied from the left-hand end of string to sub, and finally a terminating ASCII null is added. Notice, though, that since no value is returned by the function, there is no need for a return statement. An automatic return is executed on reaching the closing curly bracket.

Problem 1

This function is not robust. That is, if n exceeds the length of string, garbage will be transferred to sub. This won't actually do any harm because an ASCII null is transferred first, so an attempt to print sub results in the whole of the string appearing. However this is likely to lead to confusion during debugging. Modify the function so that it returns true if the substring is a valid length and false otherwise.

You can then write:

$$\text{if } (!\text{left}(a, b, 7))$$
$$\text{printf(“invalid string slice”);}$$

which will do the transfer *and* tell you if it doesn't mean anything.

Right a Bit

The equivalent function to pick up the rightmost n characters of a string is clearly going to be pretty similar:

```
right(string, sub, n)
char string[ ], sub[ ];
int n;
{
    int i;
    for (i = len(string) − n; i <= len(string); i++)
        sub[i] = string[i];
}
```

No problems at all with that. Of course, we need the len function to decide where to start. After that, every byte, including the terminating null, is copied over.

Problem 2

Write the function substring that takes an argument string, transferring its result to sub as before, but has two numeric arguments. The first defines which character to start from and the second how many to transfer. So:

```
strcpy(string, "hotdog");
substring(string, sub, 4, 2);
printf(sub);
```

would give "do".

This is BASIC's good old MID$ of course, but I've always felt the term "MID" to be quite misleading in this context, because there's no reason why MID$ should select the *middle* of a string. It can just as easily select from either end. Speaking of which, if we had written substring first, right and left could have been written more simply in terms of substring!

More About Pointers

Actually, very few C programmers would have written these string handling functions as I've shown. I've already mentioned the implicit connection between arrays and pointers. But C allows you to make this relationship explicit. A variable can be declared to be a pointer, by preceding it with an asterisk in a type declaration statement. Thus

char ∗p;

declares p to be a pointer to characters. In an assignment statement the asterisk notation is used to identify the object being pointed at. So

∗p = 0;

means "put a zero in the byte which p points to" (assuming *p* is a pointer to characters; if it points to integers, zero would be placed in a word).

Let's revise the len function in the light of this.

```
len(s)
char *s;
{
        char *begin;
        begin = s;
        while (*s++)
            ;
        return (s − begin − 1);
}
```

This is clearly a very close relative of the original len function. We're just missing a few square brackets, and we have to store the initial pointer value rather than setting a counter to zero.

Left Again

Let's rewrite left in the same way:

```
left(string, sub, n)
char *string, *sub;
int n;
{
        while (n−−)
            *sub++ = *string++;
        *sub = 0;
}
```

Isn't that neat? I've changed the control structure to a while loop. It just seems more natural; *n* is decremented until it's zero, so the loop is executed *n* times. Inside it, characters are passed from where string points to where sub points, and each pointer gets bumped to look at the next character. Finally the delimiter is added as before.

Further Right

A similar job on right could give:

```
right(string, sub, n)
char *string, *sub;
int n;
{
        string = string + len(string) − n;
        while (*string)
```

```
                *sub++ = *string++;
            *sub = 0;
        }
```

Again, I've altered the loop construct, and the way in which it's finished. Think about it!

Copycat

Some time back I mentioned that we would need a function called strcpy to move strings about, and another one, strcat, to concatenate two strings together into the array space of the first. Let's write strcpy:

```
        strcpy (target, source)
        char *target, *source;
        {
            while (*source)
                *target++ = *source++;
            *target = 0;
        }
```

This kind of construction should be becoming very familiar!
   Here's a possible strcat:

```
        strcat(string, extra)
        char *string, *extra;
        {
            string = string + len(string);
            while (*extra)
                *string++ = *extra++;
            *string = 0;
        }
```

The pointer into string is adjusted to point to its end, and then a string copy is performed. So we could rewrite it:

```
        strcat(string, extra)
        char *string, *extra;
        {
            string = string + len(string);
            strcpy(string, extra);
        }
```

Of course, it's left to the programmer to ensure that enough space is allocated to the string to contain the additional characters.
   Notice that in all these examples I have done arithmetic with the passed parameters with gay abandon. This is perfectly safe because, of course, I am only affecting the *local* copies of the variables.
   And now I have to tell you that we have spent much of this chapter

reinventing the wheel. Most of these functions are provided in any C function library, and are given these names as standard (except for len, which is usually called strlen; I used the BASIC terminology for easy comparison). Never mind! It's all good practice.

While I am in confessional mood, I should also warn you that the technique I've used for initialising strings is a bit sloppy. It may not work on some compilers. It is safer to use strcpy to do the job, but, of course, I didn't *have* strcpy when I first wanted to set up a string. For an alternative method, see Chapter 6.

Answers

Problem 1

Here's one solution:

```
left(string, sub, n)
char string[ ] sub[ ];
int n;
{
    int i, valid;
    valid = 1;
    for (i = 0; i < n; i++) {
        sub[i] = string[i];
        if (!sub[i])
            valid = 0;
    }
    sub[i] = 0;
    return valid;
}
```

We begin by assuming that the transfer is valid. If at some time the transfer of a null byte occurs, the valid flag is reset to zero. I've written this using arrays rather than pointers, because you're not supposed to know about pointers yet. Don't cheat!

Problem 2

This time, *I'll* cheat and use pointers:

```
substring(string, sub, start, length)
char *string, *sub;
int start, length;
{
    string = string + start − 1;
    while (length−−)
        *sub++ = *string++;
    *sub = 0;
}
```

No real surprises here; string is made to point to the beginning of the required substring (note the '−1'—a necessary fiddle factor) and then length is used as a counter to control the number of bytes transferred.

As I mentioned earlier, if substring exists, left and right are made trivial:

```
left(string, sub, n)
char *string, *sub;
int n;
    {
        substring(string, sub, 1, n);
    }
```

and

```
right(string, sub, n)
char *string, *sub;
int n;
    {
        substring(string, sub, len(string) − n + 1, n);
    }
```

My unnumbered question, "How does C allocate space to arrays passed to functions?" has a simple answer: it doesn't. All that is passed is the array name which, of course, points to the array in the calling function. That's why the called function doesn't need to know how big the array is, and, of course, the result is exactly the same as if the pointer version of the function had been used.

Incidentally, the −1 "fiddle factor" in Problem 2 is necessary only because I am modelling the **BASIC** string-handling functions, which refer to the first character of a string as datum(1) rather than datum(0) of the corresponding array. This is odd, because BASIC is perfectly happy to refer to the zeroth element of any other array! Clearly, you could revise these functions to make them a little tidier by thinking rather more consistently.

PROJECTS

1. Write a C function day() which takes a pointer *date pointing to a string giving a date, in the format "March 18 1937," and returns a pointer *day to a string that gives the corresponding day of the week.

2. Write a perpetual calendar which, given the month and year, prints out which days of that month fall on which dates, in the usual calendar format:

August						1986
SUN	MON	TUE	WED	THU	FRI	SAT
					1	2
3	4	5	6	7	8	9
10	11	12	13	14	15	16
17	18	19	20	21	22	23
24	25	26	27	28	29	30
31						

CHAPTER 6

Floats and Other Types

"She can't do Subtraction," said the White Queen. "Can you do Division?
Divide a loaf by a knife—what's the answer to that?"

Through the Looking Glass

So far, I've limited the variable types discussed to int and char. There are a number of others, but not all C compilers support all of them. Here's the rest of the full set:

float

This is the numeric form familiar to all BASIC programmers. It allows the representation of everthing from huge numbers to tiny fractions. The exact range and precision of the representation is a function of the particular implementation. Often you'll get about 6 significant figures (decimal) and a largest representable value in the region of 10^{38}.

double

This is a second form of float, which gives a greater precision.

Qualifiers for int

There are three subtypes of integer: short, long, and unsigned.

Short and long are fairly obvious; they simply allocate less or more space to the variable. For example, you might find that a compiler that allocates 16 bits to an int will allocate 8 bits to a short and 32 bits to a long. However, there is nothing in the language definition which says this has to be the case. Effectively, the options are there for compiler designers to make the best use of their target machines, and subsequently to allow the applications programmer (you and me) the same privilege. So if, on a particular machine, short doesn't make much sense, it will probably be interpreted as an ordinary int. (Not to interpret it at all would be dangerous, because it would lead to a lack of portability; but turning it into an int can't do any harm. If there was space for a particular variable in a short, it must fit in an int.)

The unsigned form needs a little more explanation. As I've said previously, a conventional 16 bit int can hold any integer in the range -32768 to 32767, which is 65536 different values. If it's assumed that the sign is always positive, these values could just as well be 0 to 65535. The unsigned form allows you to tell the compiler that you want to think about the number as always being positive, and you get a doubled maximum value as an advantage.

In a type declaration, you can miss-out the word int for these subtypes. For example

```
unsigned pos_value;
short flag;
long big_one;
```

Signs and Shifts

I mentioned earlier that a shift operation does not always have the same effect. For an ordinary int, a division by two is performed regardless of the sign, which means in practice that the senior bit of the word is propagated right, so that the sign is preserved. However, if an unsigned int is shifted right, zeros will fill the vacated bits to the left, regardless of the original value of the high order bit. This makes perfectly good sense, because the concept of "sign" has effectively been suspended.

However, what happens if you want to shift right a character? Some systems see a character as being signed, in which case the same rules apply as for an int; while others assume it is unsigned. The story gets even more confusing. When arithmetic is performed on a char, the char is automatically promoted to an int. Thus, in a system that thinks about chars as signed, the senior bit of the char will be propagated left throughout the word, potentially leaving you with a pile of 1's that you didn't have to start with! In such systems, the "unsigned char" type is supported. There are some examples in this book (in particular in Chapter 14) where this declaration does matter. I have used only the "char" type throughout, but if your compiler supports the "unsigned char" type you will have to use that instead.

Register Variables

There is one final subtype which can be an int or char. For example

register int *n*;
register char *c*;

So far as the logic of the program is concerned, *n* is an ordinary int and *c* is an ordinary char; but the compiler is requested to leave *n* and *c* in registers in the m.p.u. whenever possible. Since that saves getting them from main memory when they're needed, the program will be speeded up somewhat if *n* and *c* are very frequently used.

This is another way in which C allows you to make the best possible used of the hardware, but it doesn't necessarily follow that the hardware is cooperative. For instance, most microprocessors have very few general purpose registers (maybe only one) which would mean that values declared as register would have to be swapped in and out of memory just as much as ordinary variables. So this subtype may not be implemented or (better) simply ignored.

Declaring Structures

It's possible to combine the basic types into *structures*. For example, suppose that you want to set up a stores catalog of some kind. Each entry will contain an item number, a description, a price and a number in stock. (In practice, there would be other factors to consider but this will do for our example.)

You can write:

```
struct cat_entry {
    int item_no;
    char description[30];
    float price;
    int stock_level;
};
```

This sets up a structure called cat_entry consisting of an int called item_no, a 30 byte array called description, a floating point number called price, and another int called stock_level. Notice the semicolon *after* the closing curly bracket. A structure definition is one of only two places you'll see this syntax.

Having defined what a cat_entry is, it's easy to tell C what a catalog is:

```
struct cat_entry catalog[200];
```

That is, catalog is an array of 200 elements, each of which has the cat_entry structure.

So cat_entry has become just another type, albeit rather a complicated one. That means there's nothing to stop me declaring a pointer to objects of type cat_entry:

struct cat_entry *p;

and I can now use p to point anywhere I like in the catalog as we shall see later. If you can't wait, see Chapter 11.

Defining Your Own Types

Defining structures comes close to defining completely new types. Well, you can do that, too, with a typedef statement. For instance, suppose you want to use a number of dates within a program. Months are simply identified as the numbers 1 to 12, so they're obviously ints, and you could declare them as such. But wouldn't it be nice if there was a *type* month which had this characteristic? It's easily organised.

typedef int month;

declares int and month to be equivalent. So now you can write

month date1, date2;

and date1 and date2 are declared to be of type month and so are ints.

Better yet, cat_entry could be given a synonym in the same way:

typedef struct cat_entry catalog;

and then

catalog unipart[5000], great_universal_stores[2000];

None of this provides you with any new programming tools. It isn't intended to. What it *does* achieve is a readability unattainable in BASIC. Just think about the arrays you'd need in BASIC to set up the Unipart and GUS catalogs. It certainly wouldn't be so clear what was going on, even if you'd written the program yourself.

Constants and Initializers

I've skated over the setting up of numeric constants so far, largely because, where we've done it, it's been exactly the same as the BASIC equivalent. So

int x;
x = 1;

will set x to 1, as you'd expect, and

float *pi*;
pi = 3.142;

sets *pi* to 3.142.

The exponent form for large or small numbers is also allowed.

float very_big_number;
very_big number = 1.3*e*9;

will allocate 1,300,000,000 to the variable.

Character Constants

We've spent some time looking at string constants, and you might imagine that a C character can be seen simply as a string of length 1. However, this isn't so, because a string of length 1 occupies 2 bytes, the second containing the null delimiter. So we need a way of allocating a value to a single byte. It's done like this:

char *c*;
c = '*A*';

In other words, when you use single quote marks you are setting the value of a single byte; double quote marks identify a string, as we've seen before.

Handling Control Characters

Control characters are those that have some effect (on a printer, say) but don't actually print a symbol. And if you can't print it, how can you put it between quote marks? Of course, you can't.

There are two ways around this. The first is the equivalent of BASIC's CHR$ function. For example

char bell;
bell = 7;

sets the character variable 'bell' to ASCII 7, which if output to a printer (yes, I *know* we don't know how to do that yet; see Chapter 12) will usually make some kind of noise.

However, there are some control characters that are so commonly needed that C makes special provision for them. Each is preceded by a backslash (\), called, in the jargon, an *escape*. An *escape sequence* consists of backslash followed by a single character, or a 3 (or fewer) digit octal number. In any event, C recognizes the whole sequence as a single char. Here's the complete set:

n   newline
t   tab

\b	backspace
\r	carriage return
\f	form feed
\\	backslash
\'	single quote
\ddd	octal number
\0	ASCII null

For example you could write:

> printf("This is \n on three \n lines");

The resulting display would be:

This is
on three
lines

Any subsequent printf will cause output to follow the word 'lines' because there's no \n at the end of the string. Similarly

> printf("Attend to printer!\7\7\7");

would send the message and ring the bell three times. I stress that the '7' here is an octal not a decimal number (although 7 octal happens to equal 7 decimal) and I'll have more to say on that subject shortly.

   Note that ASCII null is given an escape sequence. So when you're searching for the end of a string you can write

> while(*p != '\0') {
>
>   . . .
>
> }

for instance. Because \0 happens to *be* zero (i.e., false) I've gotten away so far with the equivalent form

> while(*p) {
>
>   . . .
>
> }

which I personally prefer. But you may feel that it is too cryptic and that the expanded form is more meaningful. Anyway, you are likely to come across both constructs in other people's code and should therefore be familiar with them.

Define Your Own Constants

C is unusual in having a preprocessor built into its compilation system. That is to say, the source program is (or can be) mucked about with *before* the compiler gets to play with it.

All preprocessor commands are preceded by the '#' symbol. Here I want to deal with only one of them, and that in its simplest form:

#define

This command can be used to tell the preprocessor to replace any set of symbols in the source listing by any other set of symbols. For example

#define   NULL   '\0'

will replace every occurrence of the word NULL with the escape sequence for an ASCII null. Now I could write

```
while(*p != NULL) {
    . . .
}
```

which is clearer than either of the previous forms. Notice that it is conventional (but not obligatory) to write defined symbol sequences in upper case. This is simply an aid to reading a C program. A #define can appear anywhere inside a program, although it will usually be at the beginning. Obviously, it will be effective only on statements that appear after it.

Variable Constants

Very often you'll need to declare an array whose size may vary from time to time. For example it might be a disk buffer, whose size is determined by the disk subsystem itself. Even an upgrade from double to quad density storage would affect it. Ordinarily, that means laboriously going through the program, looking for all references to 256 (or whatever) then making sure that this particular 256 really is a reference to the disk buffer size, and changing it to 512 (or whatever).

The wise C programmer doesn't do that and writes

#define D_B_SIZE 256

and then, for instance

char disk_buffer[D_B_SIZE];

and

```
for (p = 0; p < D_B_SIZE; p++) {
    . . .
}
```

and so on. This way, a change in hardware necessitates only some minor tinkering with a few #define's at the beginning of the program. Neat isn't it?

#include

It well may be convenient to hold a file of such definitions and then to combine it with the source code before compilation. The "#include" preprocessor command provides a simple way of doing just that. For example, if you have a file that contains all the necessary constants for your system (number of columns and rows on the VDU display, memory capacity, buffer sizes and so on) called config.dat, then you combine this with a program by writing:

```
#include ⟨config.dat⟩
main()
{
        :
        :
```

Some systems use double quotes rather than angle braces:

```
#include "config.dat"
```

Strictly speaking, the uses of braces and quotes are distinct: they indicate where the include file is. However, this depends to some extent on the implementation, so check your manual.

As a general rule, all your programs should begin:

```
#include ⟨stdio.h⟩
```

because there is, almost invariably, a file by this name that holds a number of standard definitions such as

```
#define      NULL '\0'
#define      TRUE 1
#define      FALSE 0
```

which you can then make use of without redefinition.

Octal and Hexadecimal Constants

There are times when a constant, although numeric, doesn't *really* represent a number and isn't a character either. The mask patterns of the logical operations in Chapter 4 are good examples. In the answers to the problems I considered it worthwhile pointing out that $129 = 10000001$ binary, and $224 = 11100000$ binary, for instance. That was because it was the *bit patterns* rather than the numbers they represent which were significant. So, in cases like these, it would be nice to have a format that translates to binary more easily than decimal does. C allows us to declare constants in either base 8 (octal) or base 16 (hexadecimal). In the former case, each digit can be directly encoded from a group of 3 bits, and in the latter case, groups of 4 bits are used, as shown in Table 6.1.

TABLE 6.1. Octal and Hex to Binary Conversions

Octal	Binary	Hexadecimal	Binary
0	000	0	0000
1	001	1	0001
2	010	2	0010
3	011	3	0011
4	100	4	0100
5	101	5	0101
6	110	6	0110
7	111	7	0111
		8	1000
		9	1001
		A	1010
		B	1011
		C	1100
		D	1101
		E	1110
		F	1111

So, for example, the pattern 10000001 can be seen as

$$10 \quad 000 \quad 001$$

$$2 \quad\quad 0 \quad\quad 1 \quad\quad \text{octal}$$

or

$$1000 \quad 0001$$

$$8 \quad\quad 1 \quad\quad \text{hex}$$

Note that, in both cases, the grouping takes place from the right, although, since there happen to be 8 bits, this is not obvious in the hexadecimal case.

This is not the place to discuss in detail why these conversion techniques work, and for the purpose in hand it doesn't matter. However, if you're unfamiliar with binary, octal, and hexadecimal notations, there is a plethora of books that handle the subject. Often they're on their way to a discussion of machine code for a particular machine, so look for a machine code book for your computer.

C needs a way to distinguish between decimal, octal, and hexadecimal constants. If there is a leading zero, the constant is taken as octal. If there is a leading zero followed by an 'x' the constant is hexadecimal. Thus

$$\text{mask} = 129;$$
$$\text{mask} = 0201;$$

and

$$\text{mask} = 0x81;$$

are all equivalent statements. The 'x' may be upper or lower case, as may the letters A–F which encode the bit patterns from 1010 to 1111 in hexadecimal form.

Initializers

It's possible (at least, in full implementations of C) to initialize the value of a variable when you declare it. For instance

$$\text{int } t = 7;$$

is equivalent to

$$\text{int } t;$$
$$t = 7;$$

An array can be initialized in a similar way.

$$\text{int discount}[3] = \{0, 7, 12\};$$

is equivalent to

$$\text{int discount}[3];$$
$$\text{discount}[0] = 0;$$
$$\text{discount}[1] = 7;$$
$$\text{discount}[2] = 12;$$

It's evident that this is a convenience rather than a strict necessity, and a number of popular C compilers don't support initialization. I've never lost any sleep over this lack, but you should remember that if your system *does* support initializers, and you want to port a program on to somebody else's computer, you may have to rewrite a few bits of code. Incidentally, the array initialization construction is the second (and last) time you'll see a semicolon after a closing curly bracket.

Initializing Pointers

In our discussion on pointers in Chapter 5, we set up their initial values implicitly. For example

$$\text{int } a[50], *p;$$
$$p = a;$$

will make p point to the beginning of the array a, because a is itself a pointer to the beginning of the array.

However, C allows us to determine the actual machine address of a variable, by preceding it with '&'. For instance

$$\text{int fred, } *p;$$
$$p = \&\text{fred};$$

p is now a pointer to fred. If we needed to know exactly where in the machine

C had decided to allocate space to fred, we need only print out *p*. So it's convenient to pronounce '&' as 'address of'.

Note that it is possible to talk about "the address of the zeroth element of array *a*" as '&*a*[0]'. This is, of course, exactly the same as *a*, according to our definition of an array name. So

$$\text{int } a[50], *p;$$
$$p = a;$$

is exactly equivalent to

$$\text{int } a[50], *p;$$
$$p = \&a[0];$$

While it's not clear why you would want to use the latter form, it *is* evident that

$$p = \&a[49];$$

could be useful, if you want to search the array from top to bottom, as in

```
int a[50], *p, *q;
p = a;
q = &a[49];
while (*p++ != *q--)
    ;
```

Problem 1

What does the above piece of code do?

Declaring Function Types

Since a function attains the value it returns, it ought to be no surprise that the type of a function (i.e., the type of the object it returns) should be declared. The real surprise is that we haven't needed to do this so far. The reason is that C assumes a function returns an int unless you tell it otherwise.

Most of the time, that's exactly what a function *does* return, so there's no problem. Even if it returns a char, nothing unpleasant will happen because a char is promoted to an int when you do anything with it.

However, let's consider a function find_char, which accepts a pointer to a string and a character, and returns a pointer to the first occurrence of the specified character in the string

```
find_char (s, c)
char *s, c;
{
    while(*s++ != c)
        ;
    return (s - 1);
}
```

Nothing remarkable about that. A calling routine might be

```
main()
{
    char message[30], *find_char(), *p;
    :
    :
    strcpy (message, "this is a test");
    :
    :
    p = find_char(message, 's');
    :
    :
}
```

The important thing to notice is the declaration of find_char. It's identified as a pointer to characters O.K., but note the brackets following its name. These indicate that it *is* a function, not a simple variable.

Answers

Problem 1

On completion of the loop, p will point one higher, and q one lower, than the first symmetrically positioned pair of values. Thus if the array appears as

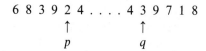

$$6\ 8\ 3\ 9\ 2\ 4\ \ldots\ 4\ 3\ 9\ 7\ 1\ 8$$

p and q will end up pointing one position past the 9's which are 4 cells from either end of the array.

CHAPTER 7

Input

The last time she saw them they were trying to put the dormouse in the teapot.

Alice's Adventures in Wonderland

I've said nothing at all yet about how to get things *into* the machine in C, and little enough about getting stuff out again. I'll remedy these omissions in the next two chapters.

Primitive Input

At the simplest level, C provides a function getchar which returns the next character input from the keyboard. At least it's usually from the keyboard, but most C systems define standard input and output devices that very easily can be altered. The default is normally the console (keyboard and monitor) and that's what I'll assume for the time being.

So we'll build a few input functions using getchar, by way of illustration.

Get a Bufferfull

The most obvious extension to getchar is to allow a set of characters to be input to a buffer for subsequent processing. We'll write a function getbuf for this.

First, we must decide how big the buffer should be, and what character is to be recognised as a delimiter. The obvious answers are "the width of the screen" and "ASCII carriage return," but remember that C encourages us not to take such decisions until the last possible moment, so we can make them the subject of preprocessor commands

#define BUFSIZE 40
#define DELIM 13

and ignore the problem altogether within the function.

Here's a first attempt at the function:

```
getbuf(buffer)
char *buffer;
{
      char *bptr;
      for (bptr = buffer; bptr < buffer+BUFSIZE; bptr++) {
            *bptr = getchar();
            if (*bptr == DELIM)
                  return;
      }
}
```

A pointer to a buffer allocated in the calling function is passed to getbuf, a local pointer is set up, and as each character is input it is passed to the buffer via this pointer. When exactly BUFSIZE characters have been transferred, control passes back to the calling function, unless the DELIM character is identified first, in which case a return is executed immediately.

Notice that we couldn't then write something like

printf(buffer);

because we haven't tagged a NULL on to the end of the character sequence, so it isn't a string.

In any event, most C programmers would use a while loop rather than the for construct, in a rather novel way

```
getbuf(buffer)
char *buffer;
{
      int num_chars;
      num_chars = 0;
      while ((*buffer++ = getchar()) != DELIM && num_chars <
            BUFSIZE) num_chars++;
      *buffer='\0';
}
```

The variable num_chars acts as a counter to determine how many characters have been transferred so far. The while condition needs some explanation.

Let's recreate it in stages. First, we're looking for a delimiter every time we get a character. So you might expect a construction like

while (getchar( ) != DELIM)

Unfortunately, although the input character is tested against DELIM correctly, it is then thrown away, because I haven't asked for it to be put anywhere. So we need to be able to do two things at once: store the character away *and* test to see if it terminates the loop.

It should come as no surprise that we *can* do this; after all, an auto-increment in an assignment also constitutes a double operation in the same statement. Problem 1 in Chapter 5 illustrates a similar feature because the 'left' process is performed and its validity tested at the same time. What this boils down to is that any assignment can be used *inside* an expression. So it should be possible to write

while (c = getchar( ) != DELIM)

This is legitimate C, but it won't do what you expect! It will test the input character against DELIM and then throw it away. It *won't* assign it to c. This is true because '!=' has a higher priority than '=', so the test is done first, by which time it's too late to do the assignment! So you must bracket the assignment

while ((c = getchar( )) != DELIM)

Now we begin to have something that looks like the final construction. It's only necessary to replace 'c' with '*buffer++' (because the character is to be transferred to where buffer is pointing and then the pointer is to be incremented), and to tag on the second condition for the loop to continue (num_chars < BUFSIZE). In the body of the loop it remains only to increment num_chars. Before returning, I've added a NULL to the buffer so that it can be handled as a string. I also could have added

return num_chars;

so that the function gives you the number of buffered characters.

Operator Precedence

This discussion has highlighted a problem that I've so far ignored. What order do operations occur in? For instance, I've just used the construction

*buffer++

Does this mean "increment buffer and then use it as a pointer" or "use buffer as a pointer and then increment it"? We've used it to mean the latter and that is correct. It's not surprising either, because it is, after all, the post-increment form. If I'd used

*++buffer

the increment would have occurred first, and we'd get one spurious character at the beginning of the buffer.

However, suppose you wanted to increment not the pointer, but what the pointer points to:

$$(*buffer)++$$

would do the job.

Thus, as with BASIC, if you want to force an order of operations you use brackets to bind the relevant operators and operands more tightly than is usual. The difference is that C has some unique operators and it's necessary to remember their precedence. The golden rule is "If in doubt use brackets."

The order of precedence of those operators we've met so far is:

```
( )    [ ]
* (pointer)   & (address)   − (negative)   !   ~   ++   −−
* (multiply)   /   %
+       −(minus)
>>       <<
<     >     <=     >=
==     !=
& (bitwise AND)
^                              On some systems these have equal precedence
|
&&
||                             On some systems these have equal precedence
=    +=    −=    *=    /=    %=    >>=    <<=    &=    ^=    |=
```

The highest priority operators are those at the top of the list, and those on the same lines have equal priority. The order of evaluation of equal precedence operators *is* defined but it isn't *always* left to right. My view is that it's less complicated to use brackets than to remember a fairly obscure set of rules which you stand a chance of misinterpreting anyway.

Problem 1

Revise getbuf to produce a string whose ASCII codes are each one greater than those of the input symbols. Thus if you input '*abcd*' the string '*bcde*' is generated. Although it could be argued that there's the germ of a cypher generating program in this exercise, my reason for suggesting it is that it really does test your grasp of operator precedence rules.

Strings to Numbers

Let's assume that the string created by getbuf is actually to be treated as a number. We'll write a function atoi which converts the first sequence of digits it finds in the string to an integer. This function is almost certainly in your library, but it's an interesting example anyway. We'll allow a fairly free format; the number may be preceded by any number of spaces followed by an optional sign symbol, followed by the digits and then any non-digit. So

$$137d$$
$$137$$
$$+137?$$

will all be interpreted as "one hundred thirty seven." In the second case, there is nothing following the number, but there will at least be the ASCII NULL terminating the string, so that can be used.

At least, that's our final aim. My opinion is that you should never make things difficult until you've made them simple, so we'll start with a much easier problem. We'll assume that the integer is always signed, and that the pointer passed to the function is pointing at the sign. This function is going to be called by atoi so I'll give it another name, convert.

```
convert(p)
char *p;
{
    int result, sign, forever;
    result = 0;     sign = forever = 1;
    if (*p++ = '-')
        sign=-1;
    while (forever) {
        result += (*p++ - '0');
        if (!isdigit(*p))
            return(result * sign);
        result*= 10;
    }
}
```

Even this function requires quite a bit of explanation. First, look at the initialisation

$$sign = forever = 1;$$

Of course I could have written

$$sign = 1;   forever = 1;$$

but the former arrangement is another example of writing an assignment inside an expression. The variable sign is set to 1 to indicate a positive value. The first test

$$if (*p++= '-')$$
$$sign =-1;$$

simply resets this to −1 if the number is, in fact, negative, and at the same time bumps the pointer so that it's looking at the first digit.

Next, an endless while loop is entered. To see what happens here, think about an example, +31, say. The relevant chunk of memory looks like this:

Characters	+	3	1	\0	or any other
Decimal values	43	51	49	0	non-digit

↑
p

So result has 51 − 48 (ASC11 0) = 3 added to it and the pointer is bumped. The new value pointed to is tested to see if it is a digit (this assumes the presence of a function isdigit which returns true if its argument is a digit). It is, so result is multiplied by 10, giving 30 so far. Now we're at the top of the loop again, so 49 − 48 = 1 is added to result, giving 31. By this time, p is pointing to the ASCII null (or whatever terminates the number) so result * sign is calculated and returned. Since sign is 1, this value is 31, which is correct! Had a minus sign preceded the number, sign would have been set to −1 and −31 would have been returned.

This algorithm has two requirements for it to work correctly. First, as I've already pointed out, there must be a sign preceding the digits, and second, there must be at least one digit, because the first character in the string is added into result (less the 48 which turns it into a number) *regardless* of what it is. This means that atoi must ensure that these conditions exist before calling convert. So we'll write a function called setup which takes two arguments that are pointers to the "raw data" buffer and a character array called num. The effect of setup will be to create from buffer a string in num that is acceptable to convert. It also will return 1 or 0 depending on whether it can do this successfully or not. So atoi itself is trivial.

```
atoi(buffer)
char *buffer;
{
        char num[BUFSIZE + 1];
        if (!setup(buffer, num)) {
                printf("Not an integer");
                exit(0);
        }
        return convert(num);
}
```

But, of course, we've still got setup and isdigit to write.

```
setup(buffer, num)
char *buffer, *num;
{
        while (!isdigit(*buffer))
                if (!*buffer++)
                        return 0;
        if (*(buffer − 1) == '−')
```

```
                strcpy(num, buffer − 1);
            else {
                strcpy(num, " + ");
                strcpy(num, buffer);
            }
            return 1;
    }
```

First we bump along, looking for the first digit. If we fail to find one before the terminating null, there isn't a number to play with so we return 0. If the preceding character was a minus sign, we can simply copy the string from the sign onwards. Otherwise, we add a ' + ', and then concatenate the digits on to it. That's why num is dimensioned to BUFSIZE+1; there's a chance that the buffer contains only digits, which means that we would need one more byte for the sign. Now for isdigit.

```
            isdigit(c)
            char c;
            {
                if (c >= '0' && c <= '9')
                    return 1;
                else
                    return 0;
            }
```

That's pretty self-explanatory. Notice that I *could* have written

$$\text{if } (c >= 48 \text{ \&\& } c <= 57)$$

but it is then less clear to anyone reading the code (including yourself in a month's time!) that c is representing a digit. I adopted the same philosophy in convert when I wrote

```
            while (forever) {
                result += (*p++ − '0')
```

Again, I could have replaced '0' with 48 (or, come to that, 0x30), but it just gives you one more problem to consider. When you're writing (or reading) code as concise as that which can be produced in C, the fewer extra headaches generated the better.

A Feeble Excuse

Now I have to admit that what I have just produced is not a paragon of professional code. If you doubt me, grub around in your standard library of functions and you'll almost certainly find a version of atoi which is about 9 lines long and calls no other functions at all! My excuse is that, at least at this stage, I am not setting out to write immaculate, economical code, but rather to get across some ideas that are quite sophisticated enough without the added encumbrance of ensuring that the resulting functions are pretty.

scanf

Getchar isn't the only way to grab things from the outside world. There's a function called scanf which does the job in a way that mirrors the operation of printf.

For example, I could write

scanf("%4d   %c   %2d", &a, &letter, &n);

assuming that *a*, letter and *n* have been declared

int *a, n*;
char letter;

Then if the input string appears as

3162   *y*   47

the variable assignments that result are

a = 3162
letter = 'y'
n = 47

The most important thing to notice here is that *all* the arguments to scanf are *pointers*. So, for instance, it's the address of *n*, *not n* itself, which is passed to the function. In the example, I've made the field widths match the corresponding numbers in the control string (i.e., the string argument of the function). However I could have written

scanf("%d   %c   %d", &a, &letter, &n);

and C will use the delimiting spaces (any number of them) to determine the field widths, so that the effect is exactly the same.

However, if there are no spaces in the input line (so that it reads 3162y47), the first form of the statement will work correctly but the second will not.

It's easy to see that scanf could be built from getchar, getbuf, and atoi, but it's a fairly complex function, and since it's usually present in the library, I won't give an implementation here. In any event, what I have presented so far is incomplete and I shall have more to say later.

Answers

Problem 1

```
getbuf1(buffer)
char *buffer;
{
    int num_chars;
    num_chars = 0;
    while((*buffer++ = getchar()) != DELIM && num_chars <
        BUFSIZE) {
        num_chars++;
        (*(buffer - 1))++;
    }
    *buffer = '\0';
}
```

Don't forget that, inside the loop, buffer is pointing one element too far along the string, so we want to point at (buffer − 1). Then it's what *that* points at that is to be incremented.

PROJECT

Write a substitution cypher program. On first running, this should request as input a permutation of the alphabet, for example

"QWERTYUIOPASDFGHJKLZXCVBNM"

Then it should allow you to repeatedly input messages, and print out their encoded forms, obtained by replacing each letter by the corresponding one in the permuted alphabet. For example the input "C PROGRAM" should become

E HKGUKQD.

CHAPTER 8

Output

The first thing she heard was a general chorus of "There goes Bill!" then the Rabbit's voice alone—"Catch him, you by the hedge!" then silence, and then another confusion of voices—"Hold up his head—Brandy now—Don't choke him—How was it, old fellow? What happened to you? Tell us all about it!"

Alice's Adventures in Wonderland

We'll now turn out attention to more ways of getting the machine to talk to us. First . . . .

More about printf

There are a number of output format specifiers which can be used in the control string that I haven't mentioned yet. So far, we only have d (convert to decimal) and c (print as a single character). Others are

o : convert to octal
x : convert to hexadecimal
u : convert to unsigned decimal
s : print as a string
f : convert to decimal (from floating point)

So you could write

printf("%s%6.3f", p, x);

If p is a pointer to the string "First value is:" and x holds the value 5.813, you'll get the display

First value is: 5.813

Notice that I've specified the length of the floating point value (6 characters, 3 of them decimal places), but left C to make up its own mind about the length of the string. This clearly presents no problem, because C knows where the string ends from the terminating null. However, C will convert the floating point number to a string before printing it, so the same should be true for the f conversion (and, indeed, all the others). Indeed, this is the case, but, of course, if you omit a field length specifier the resulting layout is unpredictable.

Justification

Notice that in the above example, the system provides a leading space before '5.813' to make up the full six characters. In other words the number is pushed as far right as possible (i.e., right justified). It is possible to force left justification by preceding the length specifier with a minus sign like this, for instance,

printf("%s%-6.3f", p, x);

which, for the above example, would produce

First value is:5.813

Printing to Memory

There's a function sprintf that acts like printf except that the data it assembles isn't output at all, but passed to a string. So, if n contains 7 and hex contains

3AD2

$$\text{sprintf}(b, \text{``}\%3d\%5x\text{''}, n, \text{hex});$$

will place in the character array (b) the string

7 3AD2

Why should this be useful? Let's clarify things with a simple example. Suppose that you're doing some monetary calculations. Working in cents, you could treat all variables as ints, but when a result is output you'd like it to appear as \$38.73 (or whatever) rather than 3873. We could write a function print-money that accepts an int representing a number of cents in this way, and outputs it conventionally in dollars and cents:

```
printmoney(cents)
int cents;
{
        char out[8] = "        ";
        *out = '$';
        sprintf(out + 1, "%5d", cents);
        *(out + 6) = *(out + 5);
        *(out + 5) = *(out + 4);
        *(out + 4) = '.';
        printf(out);

}
```

As you see, the '$' symbol is first of all placed at the beginning of the string. The number of cents is then converted to a string of digits placed *after* this (hence the 'out + 1' in the sprintf). Next the junior two digits are shifted right to allow space for the '.' to be inserted, and the resulting string is output.

So you can see how a string can be manipulated in a very flexible way, whereas a straight printf would not have allowed such tinkering.

Primitive Output

Just as it is possible to input a character at a time with getchar, there is an equivalent function

$$\text{putchar}(c);$$

which will output the character held in c.

Given that printf and sprintf provide much more sophisticated output mechanisms, it may not be obvious why you would ever need it, however. Obviously, it must *be* in the function library, because whoever compiled the library needed it to write printf, so it is available to you whether you want it or not.

As a fairly academic example (at least apparently) we could write a function called type that makes the computer behave as a typewriter until a delimiter (referred to as DELIM) is encountered.

```
type()
{
        char c;
        while((c = getchar()) != DELIM)
                putchar(c);
}
```

That needs little comment, as no new ideas are introduced. It simply picks up a character at the keyboard and dumps it to the display until it find a delimiter. It's usefulness is not really clear, however, unless you remember that I mentioned earlier that the standard I/O devices can be altered. (I know I haven't said *how* yet.) If you could change the standard input to a disc file, for example, we could use this routine as it stands to copy the file to the screen, a very useful utility when you've forgotten which file is called what. I shall return to this problem in Chapter 12.

CHAPTER 9

More About Control Constructs

"At the end of three *yards I shall repeat them—for fear of your forgetting them. At the end of* four, *I shall say good-bye. And at the end of* five, *I shall go!"*

Through the Looking Glass

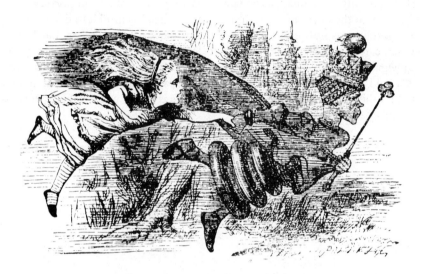

In Chapter 3, I introduced most of the control constructs C offers us. But there are others, and there also are some additional keywords that can modify the effect of the loops we've already met.

The Conditional Operator

This provides a rather cryptic form of an if ... else construct. It's general form is

expression1 ? expression2 : expression3

The effect is this. First expression1 is evaluated to true or false (non-zero or zero). If it is true, the result is the value of expression2; if false, expression3 is evaluated. So it's equivalent to

if (expression1)
expression2

else
       expression3

You can't do anything *new* with this, but you can write some more compact code. Look at the abs function of Chapter 3, Problem 1, for example. Using the conditional operator we could rewrite it like this:

```
abs(value)
int value;
{
        return (value < 0 ? -value: value);
}
```

Problem 1

Rewrite the "even" function of Chapter 4 using this construction.

Leaping out of Loops

There are occasions on which we don't want to execute a loop to completion. For example, suppose that we want to transfer the contents of one character buffer (pointed at by p) to another (pointed at by q), and that normally there are 100 characters to transfer.

```
for (i = 0; i < 100; i++)
        *q++ = *p++;
```

will do the job. However suppose that if an ASCII null is encountered we don't need to transfer the remaining characters. We can write

```
for (i = 0; i < 100; i++) {
        if (!*p)
                break;
        *q++ = *p++;
}
```

The keyword 'break' has the effect of breaking out of the smallest enclosing loop. It doesn't matter what kind of loop it is; a 'while' or 'do_while' can equally easily be exited with 'break'.

Continuing

It's also possible to jump to the end of a loop without leaving it. In other words you can conditionally bypass a chunk of the code in the loop. For example, suppose that we want to modify the above code so that any zeros in the source array are not transferred to the target array. This will do the job:

```
for (i = 0; i < 100; i++) {
    if (!*p)
        break;
    if (*p++ == '0')
        continue;
    q++ = *(p-1);
}
```

The 'continue' tells the system to skip around the remainder of the loop (in this case just '$q++ = *(p-1)$;') but to stay within the loop. That way p is incremented on every pass through the loop, but q is changed only when a non-ASCII zero is identified so that there are no gaps in the array q. Note that the character to be transferred is pointed to by $p-1$ (not p) because p already has been incremented.

As a rule, 'break' and 'continue' do not provide mechanisms that cannot be modelled in other ways. Usually, though, the alternatives to their use require complex conditions in the loop control expressions, and this leads to code that is difficult to read. In fact, the above two examples each can be handled quite easily without these two keywords. You might like to consider how! As elsewhere in C programming, experience gives you a feel for what construct is most natural in a given circumstance. This is what you should strive for. If code "feels" right it's probably easy to read, and *may* even work!

Multiway Switches

There are occasions on which it is useful to take one of several actions on the basis of a test. The 'if .. else' construct allows only two courses of action directly, although more can be dealt with by nesting, like this:

```
if (condition1)
    action1
else
    if (condition2)
        action2
    else
        if (condition3)
            action3
        etc...
```

This is generally a pretty untidy method of dealing with the problem though. C provides a mechanism for dealing directly with multiway branches, called the switch statement.

A typical example of its use might be in a menu driven data management program. The user is to have the following menu displayed.

1. Create file
2. Add entry

3. Delete entry
4. Edit entry
5. Search file
Enter choice (1–5):

There will be five functions that perform each of the listed tasks, and a function called menu which prints out the above display and returns the value entered by the user.

Here's how switch could be used to handle the situation.

```
switch (menu()) {
    case '1' : create();
            break;
    case '2' : add();
            break;
    case '3' : delete();
            break;
    case '4' : edit();
            break;
    case '5' : search();
            break;
    default : error = 1;
            printf("Invalid entry\n");
            break;
}
```

It's fairly self-explanatory. If menu returns '1', create is called; if '2' is returned, add is called and so on. But note that the code is executed from wherever the block is entered onwards, unless a 'break' is encountered. Thus if the breaks were removed and '3' was entered, delete, edit, and search would be called in turn, followed by the message "Invalid entry." Notice also the use of the keyword 'default'. If anything not explicitly referred to has been entered the default option is selected. This doesn't have to be the final case. In fact, there is no significance at all in the order in which the cases appear, which is why I've inserted a redundant 'break' at the end of the default code. Although it's not strictly necessary, since nothing follows it at the moment, the program might be edited later to include an extra case. Then it's easy to overlook the absence of a terminating 'break' and to get confused by the result.

Do Not Pass Go

One control mechanism I've so far avoided is the dreaded 'goto'. In most BASICs, it's difficult to avoid, but I haven't felt tempted to use it yet, and I doubt if you've noticed its absence. It *is* implemented in C. You can write

goto get_another_character

and then, somewhere else

get_another_character: c = getchar( );

or whatever. Thus the label for a goto to latch on to is just like a variable name, and the labeled line of code is separated from the label by a colon. That allows for more readable code than the cryptic

GOTO 1495

but it still *can* lead to knitting if it's used with gay abandon; and mostly you'll find you really don't need it, so it's probably best avoided. I've been writing C for about eight years and I don't remember writing a 'goto' once. It's not that I am a fanatic about goto-less programming (C tends to attract pragmatists rather than purists), just that, as I've remarked before, you should cultivate the habit of writing code in a way which *feels* natural, and as a rule 'goto' feels stilted.

About the only situation I can construct where a 'goto' would make sense to use would be a series of nested loops at the centre of which is a condition, which, if true, requires the whole block of loops to be exited. This sort of thing:

```
while(..) {
    :
    while(..) {
        :
        while(..) {
            :
            if (x < 0)
                goto out;
        }
    }
}
out: ....
```

Using 'break here wouldn't make sense, because it only breaks out of the *smallest* enclosing loop, so you would have to repeat

```
if (x < 0)
    break;
```

in each loop, and obviously that's messy.

Answers

Problem 1

```
even(n)
int n;
{
    return (n%2?0:1)
}
```

CHAPTER 10

Recursion

> *"Well, just then I was inventing a new way of getting over a gate—would you like to hear it?"*
>
> *"Very much indeed," said Alice politely.*
>
> *"I'll tell you how I came to think of it," said the Knight. "You see," I said to myself, "The only difficulty is with the feet: the head is high enough already. Now, first I put my head on top of the gate—then the head's high enough—then I stand on my head—then the feet are high enough, you see—then I'm over, you see."*
>
> *Through the Looking Glass*

Among the first things for which children are berated when they are learning their mother tongue is any attempt at a circular definition. "A chair is a chair with..." "You can't explain something by using the word you're explaining!" they're told firmly.

So it is later when they learn mathematics. "To multiply two numbers together you first multiply..." "How can we define something in terms of itself?" they're asked plaintively.

Actually, with certain restrictions, circular definitions are perfectly legitimate, and they provide a powerful tool for the programmer. An equivalent
of a circular definition is a function which calls itself. Computer scientists call
such functions *recursive*, being, like the rest of us, unhappy with the term
circular; they had the same propaganda drilled into them as tots.

Like most other languages (even BASIC!), C allows recursive function calls.
I did say there were some restrictions to consider, though. You can't write

```
recursive_function(a)
int a;
{
        recursive_function(a);
}
```

and expect anything to happen! In fact, if you try that the program goes into
an endless loop in which it calls the function, which calls the function, which
calls the function, and so on. Sooner or later you run out of memory, because
on every call the system has to remember where it must return to, so these
return addresses are stacked up until there's nowhere left to put them.

Clearly then, there must be a condition in the function definition that allows
an exit. Further, it must be possible to *meet* the condition, otherwise the
function calls itself indefinitely as before.

Factorials

Let's look at a concrete example. The factorial of a number, n (written $n!$) is
defined as:

$$n! = 1 \times 2 \times 3 \times \ldots n$$

As it happens, it's a simple matter to write a conventional loop to do this.

```
factorial(n)
int n;
{
        int result;
        result = 1;
        while (n--)
                result *= n;
        return result;
}
```

For convenience, I've started at n and worked down rather than working up
from 1.

However, we can see the idea of a factorial in a recursive way:

$$n! = n(n-1)!$$

and

$$1! = 1.$$

So, for example

$$4! = 4 \times 3!$$

and

$$3! = 3 \times 2!$$

and

$$2! = 2 \times 1!$$

and now $1! = 1$, so it follows that $2! = 2$, $3! = 6$, and finally $4! = 24$. This approach leads to the following code.

```
factorial(n)
int n;
{
    if (n == 1)
        return 1;
    return n*factorial(n − 1);
}
```

Clearly, this is a simple case, and there is no particular advantage in the recursive structure. But even so it's evident that there is a marginal simplification to be had from thinking about the problem in this apparently cack-handed way. In more complex examples, recursion can really be made to pay off!

Things with Strings

As a slightly more complex example, let's consider the problem of reversing the symbols in a string (so that "message" would become "egassem" for instance). Again, the job can be done conventionally, but it's instructive to try to think recursively with simple cases to avoid getting embroiled in the detail of more difficult practical problems. This is, after all, a new way of thinking about problem solving.

The first job is to consider the simplest case we can (the equivalent of evaluating 1! in the factorial example). We'll assume that reversing a string of length one is meaningless, so the shortest string we need consider has two characters. That's a simple exchange job; but for reasons which will become apparent later I want to introduce two extra functions called 'head' and 'tail' which return the first character and the rest of the string respectively. So 'head' of "message" is 'm' and 'tail' is "essage". (More precisely, 'tail' returns a pointer to "essage".) So in this trivial case we only need to concatenate the head on to the tail. Note though, that we won't be able to use strcat for that, because the head of the string is a single character, *not* a string. So we'll need a third subsidiary function, addchar, which will add a character to the end of a string. That's easy.

```
addchar(p, c)
char *p, c;
{
        while (*p++)
            ;
        *(p-1) = c;
        *p = 0;
}
```

So the pointer is updated until it finds the terminating null. Since it's a post increment, it actually goes one byte past this point, which is why the character is placed at the byte pointed to by $p-1$. The extra character is placed at the byte pointed to by $p-1$. A new null is added in the next byte and that's all there is to it.

While we're at it, let's deal with the other subsidiary functions:

```
head(p)
char *p;
{
        return *p;
}
```

which hardly bears comment, and

```
tail(p)
char *p;
{
        return (p + 1);
}
```

also not a masterpiece of subtlety and guile.

Armed with these tools we can get around to writing reverse:

```
reverse(p, q)
char *p, *q, *tail();
{
        if (strlen(p) == 2) {
            strcpy(q, tail(p));
            addchar(q, head(p));
        }
}
```

p and q are pointers to the source and destination strings respectively. If the source string is 2 elements long, we copy the tail of p to q (which is fine, because strcpy expects both its arguments to be pointers to strings) and then we add the head of p to the result. But if the string is longer:

```
        else {
                reverse(tail(p), q);
                addchar(q, head(p));
        }
}
```

So now we copy the *reverse* of the tail of *p* into *q*. If the string is "*abcd*," that will be "*dcb*," which will then have '*a*' tagged on to it by the addchar operation. That's why I needed the 'tail' function. It had to deal with a gradually decreasing string so that sooner or later the $strlen(p) == 2$ condition would be met and the recursion would "unwind."

Recursion is not an easy concept to grasp and I wouldn't be surprised if you were still a little suspicious of the reverse function, even if you've tried it out and found that it really does work. (You have, haven't you? There's so little trust in the world these days. ...)

So let's dry-run it with "*abcd*" just to reinforce the idea. To start with, the length of the string is greater than 2 so the program would like to take the reverse of "*bcd*" and tag on '*a*'. But it can't evaluate the reverse of "*bcd*" directly, so it calls itself again and tags '*b*' onto the reverse of "*cd*". This is directly reversible to "*dc*." On the way back, '*b*' and '*a*' are tagged on, giving "*dcba*."

Don't imagine, however, that when you're writing recursive functions, this kind of analysis is particularly useful. They're usually too complicated to think about at this level of detail. And that's precisely the point about recursion. It allows one to describe a complex process in a very tight way, which necessarily makes a dry run horrendously confused.

Back-to-Front Sentences

Let's extend this idea a little further, We'll reverse the words in a piece of text without reversing the letters in each word. So the first sentence of this paragraph would become:

> "further little a idea this extend Let's"

While this is still a pretty academic example, it's evident that we're moving towards the kind of function which could be useful in a word processing package. And, almost as a by-product, we'll have to think about an appropriate data structure for the text which isn't immediately obvious but will, as we'll see, fit very neatly with the ideas I've introduced so far.

The basic problem is that the reversal now takes place in fits and starts. Whole groups of letters are swapped about, but within words they're left alone. So it won't be convenient to see the text as a single string, because that gives no clue to the grouping involved and we would need to search for spaces to find out where the words are. Suppose each *word* is a separate string. The text can then be an array of pointers to strings, like this:

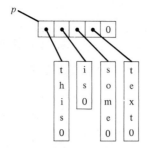

The declaration for p would be something like

$$\text{char } *p[200];$$

which sets up a 200 element array of pointers to characters. Note the declaration carefully. This is the first time we've come across such a "composite." As we shall see, much more complex ones are possible.

In and Out

To get the feel of this organization, let's write a couple of functions called *intext* and *outtext*. Intext will accept a string and form the internal structure from it, and outtext will print out such a structure. Here's the code for intext:

```
intext(s, p, text)
char *s, *p[ ], *text;
{
        int i;
        i = 0;
        while (*s) {
                p[i++] = text;
                while ((*text++ = *s++) != ' ')
                        ;
                *text++ = 0;
        }
        p[i] = 0;
}
```

The original string is pointed to by s, and the array of pointers is again referred to as *p*. Notice that intext does not need to know how big this array is (hence the null entry between the square brackets), because it expects to find out from the calling function. Text points to an area that will hold the string of strings that intext will generate.

   The outer while loop simply looks for the terminating null in the source string. Until it finds it, the current value of text is passed to an element of *p* (and the subscript is incremented), and then letters up to and including the next space are transferred. Finally a null is added to the copy in text, to turn it into a complete string. Before leaving the function, the final element of *p* is set to zero so that it can act in a similar way. Notice that a space is the only word delimiter that the routine identifies, so as things stand there must be one at the end of the string. It's easy to modify the code to see other possibilities such as exclamation point, period, and so on, or simply to strcat a space on to the source string before tinkering with it.

With this arrangement, outtext is trivial.

```
outtext(p)
char *p[];
{
      int i;
      i = 0;
      while (p[i++])
            printf(p[i-1]);
}
```

So we just print the string pointed to by each pointer in the array in turn, until we meet a zero pointer. Using a delimiting pointer in this way is a shade dodgy because there is no *invalid* pointer value; it is perfectly possible to point to *address* zero. Negative values can't be used because a pointer is (arithmetically) unsigned. However, even if the compiler assigns the variables in the calling function to low memory addresses (not, in itself, very likely), the initial value of text can't be zero unless it is the first variable assigned, which we can easily ensure isn't so.

Reversing the Text

It's probably already dawned on you that with this structure, the problem of reversing the text becomes that of reversing the pointers. What may not be so obvious is quite how simple this is. All the functions we already have are directly usable except that the parameter definitions change: wherever previously there was a character, it becomes a pointer to characters, and where there was a pointer to characters it becomes a pointer to pointers to characters.

Thus the head and tail functions are

```
head(p)
char **p;
{
      return *p;
}
```

and

```
tail(p)
char **p;
{
      return (p + 1);
}
```

Notice the '∗∗' meaning 'pointer to pointer to'. It's evident that this is what it *ought* to mean, but it is worth emphasizing given that this is the first time we've met such a double indirection.

Similar changes can be made to addchar, which I've renamed addword for obvious reasons.

```
addword (p, c)
char **p, *c;
    {
        while (*p++)
            ;
        *(p−1) = c;
        *p = 0;
    }
```

and reverse becomes

```
reverse(p, q)
char **p, **q, **tail();
    {
        if (len(p) == 2) {
            ptrcpy(q, tail(p));
            addword(q, head(p));
        }
        else {
            reverse(tail(p), q);
            addword(q, head(p));
        }
    }
```

Two new functions are needed here, because the library functions strlen and strcpy must be replaced by the functions len and ptrcpy which do equivalent jobs, but for arrays of pointers to strings.

Problem 1

Write len and ptrcpy.

Answers

Problem 1

```
len(p)
char **p;
    {
        int k;
        k = 0;
        while (*p++)
```

```
            k++;
        return k;
    }
    ptrcpy(dest, source)
    char **dest, **source;
    {
        do
            *dest++ = *source++;
        while (*source);
    }
```

These functions are very straightforward. As elsewhere, the only changes from the originals are in the extra asterisks in the parameter definitions.

PROJECT

Look up the description of a binary search in Chapter 12, and rewrite it to use recursion.

Postscript

This chapter began as an exercise in recursion and has in a sense, been subverted into an investigation into data structures. It's no less useful for that, but it is worth summing up what we've learnt in passing.

First, it's become clear that if you can do something with a datum you can do it with a pointer to that datum. In our example, the datum in question is either a character or a pointer to characters, but it could just as well have been an array of pointers to structures consisting of pointers to other structures consisting of ... well, anything you like.

Second, I built the final program from a set of functions that already had been tested in a simpler data environment, and then merely changed the parameter definitions. While this is hardly necessary in this case, certainly for the experienced programmer, it might well be a useful technique when the organisation of data becomes difficult to think about.

Third, the data structure itself is interesting. It's evident that we have, in effect, built a two dimensional array consisting of n rows for a n word sentence. However, the length of a row is not a fixed value, as it would be in a conventional array. It changes with the word length. This leads to a very compact form of data representation. We could take this idea a stage further: if a 2-D array can be seen as an array of pointers to 1-D arrays, a 3-D array is an array of pointers to 2-D arrays, a 4-D array is an array of pointers to 3-D arrays, and so on. This is how most languages implement multi-dimensional arrays anyway, but C makes the connection explicit.

CHAPTER 11

Structures

"When I use a word," Humpty-Dumpty said, in a rather scornful tone, "it means just what I choose it to mean—neither more nor less .... When I make a word do a lot of work ... I always pay it extra."

Through the Looking Glass

Back in Chapter 6, I dropped some heavy hints about the usefulness of structures, and then annoyingly said no more. I'll rectify that omission here.

Let's return, by way of example, to the store catalog entry structure which I introduced in Chapter 6:

```
struct cat_entry {
    int item_no;
    char description[30];
```

```
                float price;
                int stock_level;
        };
```

As I said then, it's easy to tell C that there's an array of such structures:

```
        struct cat_entry catalog[5000];
```

but that leaves questions such as: "How do you move records around?" and "How do you change a field of a single cat-entry?"

The answer to the first question is: "You don't." You can't see a structure as a complete entity; it has to be dealt with field-by-field. This isn't such a serious restriction as it may first appear because, more often than not, you'll want to refer to a single field; the stock level may change, for example. However, if you want to move a structure from one place to another, transferring it field-by-field is tedious but unavoidable. Also, you can't pass structures between functions. As with arrays, you can only pass pointers to them.

Playing with Structures

There are two ways to identify a structure member (or field). First, you can write

```
        structure_name.member
```

For example, the price of item 3 in the catalog would be

```
        catalog[3].price
```

Thus to remove _n_ units from the stock of item 147, I could write

```
        catalog[147].stock_level -= n;
```

which is not merely neat but very easy to follow.

However, where arrays are being used, the C philosophy is, as we've seen, to refer to their elements with pointers rather than subscripts. Also, since *only* pointers to structures can be passed between functions, we're likely to be forced into this way of thinking about such references. This leads to the second form of identification

```
        pointer_to_structure_name -> member
```

For my example, we would have to declare a pointer to structures of type cat_entry

```
        struct cat_entry *pcat;
```

Then, if pcat is pointing at catalog[147], the statement

```
        pcat -> stock_level -= n;
```

is exactly equivalent to the previous "remove _n_ units from stock" statement.

Of course, pcat could have been set up with

pcat = &catalog[147];

but it's more likely to have been determined by some search routine.

Notice, incidentally, that the "pointing to" symbol (−>) consists of the two symbols "minus" and "greater than."

It's perfectly legitimate to mix the two forms of structure reference. For instance, suppose that you want to move a structure pointed at by pcat to a structure called temp:

```
struct cat_entry catalog[500], temp, *pcat;
      .
      .
      .

temp.item_no = pcat −> item_no;
temp.description = pcat −> description;
temp.price = pcat −> price;
temp.stock_level = pcat −> stock_level;
      .
      .
```

Obviously, there would have been little point in setting up a pointer to temp simply to keep the notation consistent. There *are* times, however, when such consistency can be employed as a check on your code. This makes it easy to check that all the necessary data transfers have been made. Such "good housekeeping" practices can minimise the chances of trivial "slip of the pen" errors which can be no less tricky to find than obscure algorithmic bugs.

The Storeman's Mate

Let's pull some of these ideas together into a package that might be useful to a storeman dealing with the comings and goings of catalog items.

He'll need a menu of options such as:

Add entry to catalog
Delete entry from catalog
Alter stock level
Check price of item

and so on. We've already seen how this might be done using a switch on a function called menu which displays the menu and returns the user's choice. We'll use the same technique again:

```
struct cat_entry {
    int item_no;
    char description[30];
```

```
        float price;
        int stock_level;
} catalog[500];
main()
{
        int hell_frozen_over = 0;
        char menu();
        while (!hell_frozen_over)
            switch(menu()) {
                case '1' : add();
                        break;
                case '2' : delete();
                        break;
                case '3' : alter_stock();
                        break;
                case '4' : check_price();
                        break;
                default : exit(0);
            }

}
```

So far so simple. Notice, though, that I've introduced a small variation in the definition of cat_entry and catalog; they are achieved within the same statement. This is legitimate and convenient since it saves me writing separately:

```
        struct cat_entry catalog[500];
```

Also, notice that catalog is a global structure, since it is defined outside main. We're going to assume that it already contains all the current details for the purposes of this example, but later you'll see how it could be set up by pulling the data from some backing store, such as disk.

The menu function is straightforward enough:

```
menu()
{
        printf("options are \n");
        printf("1)Add Entry to Catalog \n");
        printf("2)Delete Entry from Catalog \n");
        printf("3)Alter Stock Level \n");
        printf("4)Check Price of Item \n");
        printf("Hit any other key to exit:");
        return (getchar());
}
```

It would, of course, be simple to add options by creating extra printfs in menu, and corresponding extra cases in the switch.

Delete

We'll start by writing the delete function, because it will force us to think a little more deeply about the organization of the catalog array. Specifically, how is an item to be indicated as being deleted? One simple possibility is to set the item_no field to zero to indicate an empty record. Thus valid numbers must be 1 or greater, which is no serious inconvenience, and the addition function can simply look for a zero item_no value to determine where to place the added record. This implies that, initially, *all* item_no fields must be set to zero; but that's a once-for-all procedure which we won't consider further. Let's make this hypothetical initialization routine do us one more favor: it will set the item_no field of the final record (catalog[499]) to −1. This will give us a dummy record at the end of the array to act as a delimiter.

```
delete()
{
        struct cat_entry *p;
        int target;
        p = catalog;
        printf("Enter item no for deletion:");
        scanf("%d", &target);
        while (p −> item_no != target) {
                if (p −> item_no < 0) {
                        printf("Not found \n");
                        return;
                }
                p++;
        }
        printf("Confirm deletion of %s(y/n)", p −> description);
        if (getchar() == 'y')
                p −> item_no = 0;
}
```

There are a few points worth commenting on here. First, the definition of p as a cat_entry structure is legitimate because every function has access to the (global) structure definition. However, p itself is local to delete. Second, remember that scanf requires *addresses* as arguments (thus '&target' not 'target'). Third, p++ will increment p by the *size* of the structure (about 38 bytes, depending on the size of your ints and floats), which is just what we want. Finally, the function prints the description associated with the item number (if it's found a match) and asks for confirmation that this item is to be deleted. Any entry other than 'y' is treated as not confirming the deletion and the function is left having taken no action. This could confuse a user whose keyboard happens to be set in upper case!

So the last line of the function might be better as:

```
c = getchar();
if (c == 'y' || c == 'Y')
    p -> item_no = 0;
```

which would require the definition of the local char variable, c.
  Incidentally, don't be tempted to write

```
if (getchar() == 'y' || getchar() == 'Y'....
```

which would call getchar *twice* so inputting two characters!
  A better alternative is to use the library function tolower which converts its
input character to lower case if necessary:

```
if (tolower(getchar()) == 'y')
    p -> item_no = 0;
```

Add

The simplest addition routine will merely look for the first zero item number
and shovel the new data into the corresponding record.

```
add()
{
    struct cat_entry *p;
    p = catalog;
    while (p -> item_no) {
        if (p -> item_no < 0) {
            printf("No room\n");
            return;
        }
        p++;
    }
    printf("Enter item number:");
    scanf("%d", &(p -> item_no));
    printf("Enter description:");
    scanf("%s", &(p -> description));
    printf("Enter price:");
    scanf("%f", &(p -> price));
    p -> stock_level = 0;
}
```

There are no new ideas or sneaky tricks here. Notice that this function will
automatically set the stock level for a new item to zero, so that alter_stock
must be called to allocate some other number here.

Problem 1

Write alter_stock and check_price.

Recursive Structures

Recall the 'sentence reversal' data structure of Chapter 10. This consisted of a vector of pointers to strings. However, this vector was sliced in two by the head and tail functions, so we could alternatively have started with two pointers, one to the head and the other to the tail. The tail would then consist of a pointer to another head/tail pair, thus:

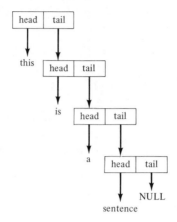

It's easy to see that this has a recursive organization because removing the top level head/tail pair has no effect on the structural appearance of the diagram. Thus we can say: "Here is a structure that consists of a pair of pointers, one of which points to a word, and the other points to another structure of the same kind."

Converting this to a C structure declaration is quite straightforward.

```
struct list {
        char *head;
        struct list *tail;
};
```

Notice, however, that this works *only* because tail is a *pointer* to a structure of type list. It is illegal to include a structure *itself* within its own definition.

Answers

Problem 1

```
alter_stock()
{
        struct cat_entry *p;
        int target, change;
```

```
        p = catalog;
        printf("Enter item number for update:");
        scanf("%d", &target);
        while (p -> item_no != target) {
                if (p -> item_no < 0) {
                        printf("Not found\n");
                        return;
                }
                p++;
        }
        printf("Enter stock change to %s:", p -> description);
        scanf("%d", &change);
        p -> stock_level += change;
}
```

The form of this function is very like that of delete. I haven't bothered to ask for confirmation that the item selected is correct, however, since the user can always enter a zero for the stock level change if necessary.

```
check_price()
{
        struct cat_entry *p;
        int target;
        p = catalog;
        printf("Enter item number for price check:");
        scanf("%d", &target);
        while (p -> item_no != target) {
                if (p -> item_no < 0) {
                        printf("Not found\n");
                        return;
                }
                p++;
        }
        printf("%s price is %f\n", p -> description, p -> price);
}
```

All these functions begin to look remarkably similar don't they? Whenever you get this sense of *deja* vu, it is a fair bet that there was an easier, or at least prettier, approach. In this example it's now clear that we keep reusing a piece of code which searches for an item number. We could write this as a function find_key which takes the target item number as an argument, and returns a pointer to the appropriate record. If it fails to find a match, it returns zero.

```
                find_key(target)
                int target;
                {
                        struct cat_entry *p;
```

```
                        p = catalog;
                        while (p -> item_no != target) {
                            if (p -> item_no < 0)
                                , return 0;
                            p++;
                        }
                        return p;
                    }
```

check-price could then be rewritten

```
check_price()
{
    struct cat_entry *find_key();
    int num;
    printf("Enter item number for price check:");
    scanf("%d", &num);
    if (find_key(num))
        printf("%s price is %f \n", find_key(num) -> description,
            find_key(num) -> price);
    else
        printf("Not found \n");
}
```

Notice the definition of find_key as a function returning a pointer to structures of type cat_entry. Look before you leap, though; this involves *three* calls to find_key, which is a slow linear search. It would have been quicker to declare an explicit pointer to cat_entry in check-price (pce, say) and then write:

```
if(pce == find_key(num))
    printf("%s price is %f \n", pce -> description, pce -> price);
```

PROJECTS

1. Currently, new entries are inserted in the catalog wherever there is space. Write an additional menu function sort that will order the entries by ascending item number.

2. Write the menu function list that will display the entire current catalog.

3. Revise find_key so that it will accept an item number *or* a description to search on.

4. Write the menu function reorder that will display all catalog entries whose stock level is below 20.

CHAPTER 12

File-handling

Alice could see, as well as if she were looking over their shoulders, that all the jurors were writing down "stupid things!" on their slates, and she could even make out that one of them didn't know how to spell "stupid", and that he had to ask his neighbor to tell him. "A nice muddle their slates'll be in, before the trial's over" thought Alice.

Alice's Adventures in Wonderland

Very early on in this book I remarked on the satisfyingly consistent nature of C compilers. Generally, sins are those of omission (float or typedef may not be implemented for instance) rather than those of juggling with the syntax or giving library functions nonstandard features.

When it comes to file-handling, however, subtle differences start to appear between implementations. This is not entirely the compiler writer's fault. The problem is that the way files are handled in a computer system is more a matter for the operating system than for *any* language (which, the operating system would like to point out, is only running *at all* because the O.S. says it can ... so there).

C works best (or, at least, most consistently) in an environment that looks pretty much like Unix, the operating system for which it was conceived; in other circumstances it may be necessary to make compromises that lead to the dreaded nonstandard feature. That is the reason this chapter appears as late as it does in this book. You will *have* to refer to your system manuals to confirm the precise details of your implementation, and you should by now be able to find your way through them with confidence.

The foregoing is also a veiled disclaimer for my benefit. The code 1 shall present has been tested on several "fairly standard" systems; but I cannot claim, as I can for the majority of code in this book, that it is therefore certain to run without modification on any other C implementation. Consequently you should treat the following with a certain amount of caution.

I/O Redirection

Most modern operating systems do not concern themselves directly with peripheral devices such as keyboards and printers, but rather with notional entities called *channels* which are then associated with specific device drivers. Thus a program communicates with a channel and the channel is linked to a device. The advantage of this mechanism is that the program need not be changed if the source of its input data changes, or its output is to be transferred to a disk file, say, rather than the printer. Only the channel/device assignment needs to be altered.

All C I/O is handled in this channel orientated way. Thus the getchar function does not (strictly) transfer a character from the keyboard to main memory; it transfers it from a *channel*, which by default is assigned to the keyboard, to main memory. This channel is referred to as stdin (for standard input). There is a corresponding channel stdout whose default assignment is the screen.

For many applications, it is only necessary to know how to reassign stdin and stdout, because very often we are simply taking a single disk file, processing it, and creating a new one; which is exactly analogous to accepting some keyboard input, processing it and displaying the results.

A typical mechanism for informing the operating system of this redirection of I/O might be

cprogram <a:data.text >b:newdata.text

which would be interpreted: "Run the program called cprogram. Take its input from a file on drive a called data.text and dump its output to a file on drive b called newdata.text."

The '<' is being used to indicate input redirection and the '>' is the corresponding symbol for output redirection.

Error Messages

There is one difficulty with this arrangement: any runtime error messages would be redirected along with the output data and the results could be somewhat mystifying. To get over this problem there is a third standard channel called stderr to which error messages are sent. This defaults to the screen, and it is usually not possible to redirect it. On some systems it is possible to *read* from stderr, in which case the keyboard is read, regardless of the setting of stdin.

Buffered File I/O

Of course, things would be a bit restricted if we could use *only* the standard channels. C provides a number of extra mechanisms for setting up and handling files from within programs. Generally these will be disk files, but, with the current vogue for screen windows, it's now common to find them also handled as separate files by the operating system.

There are a number of standard library functions that conduct the relevant bargaining with the operating system and do all the necessary internal house-keeping, such as allocating buffer space and keeping pointers to it, without involving the programmer in the gory details. They are:

fopen   :   open a channel to a file
getc   :   get a character from a channel
putc   :   send a character to a channel
fscanf :   like scanf, but access a channel rather than the keyboard
fprintf :   like printf, but access a channel rather than the screen
fclose :   flush a channel buffer and close a file

In some systems, the functions fgetc and fputc are provided as synonyms for getc and putc, so that all buffered file I/O functions start with the letter 'f'. Let's deal with each of these functions in detail.

fopen

This is used in the form:

$$cid = fopen(fname, mode);$$

fname is a pointer to a string, which is the name of the file. mode is also a string, although it will contain only a single letter:

r   if the file is opened for reading
w   if the file is to be written to (in which case any previous file of the same name is deleted first)
a   if the program output is to be appended to an existing file

fopen returns a *channel identifier* (which I've shown as cid), and all subsequent references to the file are made using this value. The programmer need never know what that value *is*, because one simply refers to 'cid'.

Actually, that isn't entirely true. Under Unix, cid is a pointer to a structure which is given the defined type FILE. This mechanism is possible only if the compiler implements typedef, so here is an obvious case where anomalies can creep in.

In other systems, it may be a pointer to an int, and is then often referred to as a file descriptor. Since Unix also uses the term file descriptor to mean something subtly different from a FILE pointer, I have chosen to use the term channel identifier (which as far as I know, nobody uses in *any* context) to allay some of the potential confusion. What it boils down to is that you will have to refer to your system manual to find out how to declare the type of cid and fopen.

Creating a File

Now all subsequent references to a file are made via the channel identifier. For instance the following code would create a file that contains the integers 1 to 100, together with their squares:

```
main()
{
    FILE *cid;
    int n;
    cid = fopen("squares.dat", "w");
    for (n = 1; n < 101; n++)
        fprintf(cid, "%d %d\n", n, n*n);
    fclose(cid);
}
```

I've assumed that cid is a pointer to FILE, which, of course, you may need to change. The call to fopen sets up a file called squares.dat for writing and returns its channel identifier in cid. Then a sequence of numbers is printed to the file using fprintf, whose format is identical to that of printf except for an extra argument (the first) which references the appropriate channel identifier. What is sent to the file is an *exact* image of what would have appeared on the screen for the equivalent printf. For example

```
1   1
2   4
3   9
4   16
5   25
```

etc., with exactly one space separating the pairs of numbers, because that's what's in the control string. I emphasize this point because the precise data format may affect the way in which it is convenient to retrieve the file. Consequently it can be a useful trick to *think* about the file organization as though the data were being sent to the screen.

Once More, with Filing

Now to get the data back again. Of course, this presents no *practical* problem at all, because whatever your operating system, it has a utility to copy files to the screen or printer. Obviously, it's worth using this to check that the file has been created correctly, but I'm more concerned here with writing a program to do the job, as another file handling exercise.

Since we know the precise nature of the file to be read, and the number of records in it, one way to handle the problem would be to write a near "mirror image" of the file creation program:

```
main()
{
        FILE *cid;
        int n, v, vsq;
        cid = fopen("squares.dat", "r");
        for (n = 1; n < 101; n++) {
                fscanf(cid, "%d %d", &v, &vsq);
                printf("%d %d", v, vsq);
        }
        fclose(cid);

}
```

There is little to comment on here, except to remind you that fscanf, like scanf, requires its arguments to be *pointers* and to say that, although a call to fclose is not perhaps an absolute necessity on input (because there's no need to flush a buffer), it is desirable, since it frees the channel identifier for subsequent use.

This solution is hardly pretty, because it can handle only this one file. It presents no problem at all to be very much more general:

```
main()
{
        FILE *in_cid, *out_cid;
        char source[20], dest[20], c;
        printf("File from:");
        scanf("%s", source);
        printf("File to:");
        scanf("%s", dest);
        in_cid = fopen(source, "r");
        out_cid = fopen(dest, "w");
        while ((c = getc(in_cid) != EOF)
                putc(c, out_cid);
        fclose(in_cid);
        fclose(out_cid);

}
```

This is (almost) a typical operating system filecopy utility. It allows us to specify where the file is to come from, and where it is to be copied to, and then picks the data off the input file character by character, looking for an end of file marker EOF, and copying each byte to the output file until it finds one.

Of course, this way of thinking forces us to name an output file even when we only want to output data to the screen. That is unlikely to be a problem (most operating systems see the console as a file anyway, and give it a name like con: or scr_) but if you want a specific 'display file on screen' utility, you need not open an output file at all. Just replace

$$putc(c, out\_cid);$$

with

$$putc(c, stdout);$$

or, come to that

$$putchar(c);$$

File Access Errors

There are several glaring omissions from the above code, all of which have to do with the problem of errors that may occur during disk reads (or writes). Sometimes such an error may relate to a hardware problem, such as disk head alignment, or physical disk damage, but there are much more mundane possibilities. For example, suppose you try to open a new file and there is no remaining space in the disk directory. The operating system will simply report its inability to set up the file. Similarly, if we attempt to open a nonexistent file for reading, much the same thing will happen. However, as I've written it, the filecopy program will plough on regardless, at best doing nothing useful and at worst leaving mayhem in its wake.

This need not happen, because fopen tells us whether it was successful in opening the file. It does this by returning a channel identifier value of zero if the file could *not* be opened for any reason.

Typically, putc and fclose also will report failure. EOF may be returned by putc, and a non-zero value by fclose.

So a more robust filecopy would be:

```
main()
{
    FILE *in_cid, *out_cid;
    char source[20], dest[20], c;
    printf("File from:");
    scanf("%s", source);
    printf("File to:");
    scanf("%s", dest);
    if ((in_cid = fopen(source, "r")) == 0) {
```

```
            printf("No file %s", source);
            exit(0);
      }
      if ((out_cid = fopen(dest, "w")) == 0) {
            printf("Cannot open %s", dest);
            exit(0);
      }
      while ((c = getc(in_cid)) != EOF)
            if (putc(c, out_cid) == EOF) {
                  printf("disk error");
                  exit(0);
            }
}
```

Random Access Files

So far we've treated disc files as though they were handing data to us in a fixed sequence, as though they were serial files, in fact. There's nothing inherently wrong with this, but it does mean that we're not making use of the disk drive's ability to skip between tracks at will.

As usual, C provides a library function that does most of the hard work for you. Effectively, it allows you to think about a file as a character array on disk, and it provides a mechanism for setting the "array subscript." The general form of this function is

lseek(cid, skip_bytes, start);

Its effect is to move the subscript around in the following way.

cid is the channel identifier, as before
skip bytes is the number of bytes to be skipped from:
start which is:

0   if the skip is to be computed from the beginning of the file
1   if the skip is to be computed from the current position
2   if the skip is to be computed from the end of the file

For instance

lseek(cid, 200, 0);

will set the system up so that the next getc will read the 200th byte in the file. A subsequent call

lseek(cid, 50, 1);

would arrange for byte 250 to be read next; or, of course, *written* next, with putc. Hence the obvious use of

lseek(cid, 0, 2);

which moves the subscript to the end of the file (start-2) and skips 0 bytes, thus leaving the file in the "append" state.

The type of skip_bytes varies between implementations. Often it is a long int. Sometimes it is just an int. Clearly it has to be capable of representing a fairly large number, because it defines the maximum size of a file.

Before we look at uses for the lseek function, I should issue a solemn warning: Never write to a file (having first used lseek) on a disk with *anything* interesting on it until the program has been carefully tested with a scratch disk. Obviously it's conceivable that calls to lseek can get out of hand, and data can be unintentionally overwritten.

The Square Table

Let's start with an example which, while both trivial and impractical, will serve to highlight most of the important points about using random access files. We already have a file called squares.dat which contains a list of integers and their squares. Presumably, we could use this to "look up" the square of an integer by skipping directly to the appropriate entry. The table starts:

1   1
2   4
3   9

so that a single entry consists of 4 bytes (digit, space, square, newline). In fact, this record length is implementation dependent because some systems expand the "newline" character into the combination "carriage return" and "linefeed," giving a total length of 5 bytes.

Assuming the 4 byte length is correct we can find the right record for the square of n by using lseek to skip $4*(n-1)$ bytes. Except, of course, that this breaks down on the very next record:

$$4 \quad 16$$

because the record length changes. While it isn't impossible to handle variable length records randomly, it's clearly messy and it will probably involve a significant processing overhead. So rule 1 is "Stick to fixed length records if at all possible."

Problem 1

Rewrite the squares program so that each record is 10 bytes long, assuming that each terminating newline occupies a single byte.

Second Attempt

Now that we have revised the squares.dat file to have fixed length records, things are pretty straightforward.

```
main()
{
        FILE *in_cid;
        int n, skip, v, vsq;
        in_cid = fopen("squares.dat", "r");
        printf("No. to be squared"); scanf("%d", &n);
        skip = 10*(n - 1);
        lseek(in_cid, skip, 0);
        fscanf(in_cid, "%d %d", &v, &vsq);
        printf("%d squared is %d", v, vsq);
}
```

So lseek is used to set up the position in the file, and then fscanf is used to read the whole record. Of course, we need output only the second value present, but I've chosen to print both so that there is a check that the correct entry has been chosen.

Reversing the Process

Now it's evident that this example has no practical point since the problem would never be solved this way. It is worth spelling out precisely why.

First, the connection between the fields of the record is algorithmic; each field can be obtained from the other by computation. We easily can devise examples where that is not so. Our stock control structure of Chapter 11 is a case in point. There is no direct arithmetic connection between part number and price, or between price and stock level. My reason for choosing the "squares" example was simply that it could be created without a great deal of typing.

"But," you might say, "why not pull the whole file into an array to begin with, and then access that. At least for multiple interrogations the process will be faster."

Certainly that's another valid objection. It breaks down only when the file is too big to be held in main memory.

So far the purpose of simplicity, I'm asking you to suspend disbelief in these two contexts; the fields of each record are *not* arithmetically related and the file *is* larger than main memory.

Given these conditions, can we use the table backwards—that is, display the square root of a given number? Obviously, we could simply examine each record in turn until the second field of a record matches the target value. That's a linear search; we would be using the file sequentially and, consequently, slowly. A better approach would be to use a binary search. If you're unfamiliar with this algorithm, it can be stated easily like this:

Examine the middle entry in the file. If this is the target record, the job is done. If its key field is greater than the target key, the target record must lie in the bottom half of the file. Otherwise it must lie in the top half of the file. In either case half the file has been eliminated from the search, and the process is repeated, at each stage eliminating half the remaining entries.

It's easy to show that a million or so entries can be searched exhaustively with a maximum of 24 tests using this technique. Here's an implementation of the algorithm for the "square rooting" problem.

```
main()
{
     FILE *in_cid;
     int top_rec, bottom_rec, mid_rec, key, square, skip, sqrt;
     top_rec = 100; bottom_rec = 1; key = 0;
     mid_rec = 50;
     in_cid = fopen("squares.dat", "r");
     printf("Enter no. to be square rooted"); scanf("%d", &square);
     while (square != key) {
          skip = 10*(mid_rec - 1);
          lseek(in_cid, skip, 0);
          fscanf(in_cid, "%d %d", &sqrt, &key);
          if (key > square)
               top_rec = mid_rec - 1;
          else
               bottom_rec = mid_rec + 1;
          mid_rec = (top_rec + bottom_rec)/2;
     }
     printf("Square root is %d\n", sqrt);
}
```

This is a pretty transparent implementation of the algorithm. The variables top_rec and bottom_rec delimit the current search space, and mid_rec is set to the record half way between them. The record associated with mid_rec is read and the "square" field, called key, is compared with the square value which was originally entered. If key is the greater of the two, the top half of the table is eliminated by setting top_rec to mid_rec − 1. Otherwise the bottom half is ignored by making a corresponding change in bottom_rec. When key and square are equal, the while loop is left, and the first field of the current record is printed.

So as not to obscure the basic procedure, I've omitted the usual tests on fopen and fscanf. Interestingly, when I first tested the routine, it hung up. I assumed it was in an endless loop and put in extra printf's to try to identify the problem. It still hung without printing anything. It was only then I realised that the file "squares.dat" was not on the logged on disk! Had I included a test for a successful fopen, the problem would have been clear immediately. There's a moral there somewhere.

Problem 2

There *is* a condition which will lead to the while loop executing indefinitely. What is it and how can it be avoided?

Problem 3

As it stands this procedure is hardly a useful utility. However, a few quite simple modifications will turn it into one. Write the function search_file which accepts the arguments file name, number of records in the file, the record length, the position of the first byte of the key, the length in bytes of the key, and the target key. The function sets the file subscript to the target record using lseek, and returns the record number. Thus

$$n = search\_file(\text{``data''}, 2000, 25, 7, 3, test);$$

will look for the integer 'test' in bytes 7, 8, and 9 of a 2000 record file called "data," each of whose records is 25 bytes long.

Answers

Problem 1

It's necessary only to change the fprintf control string

$$fprintf(cid, \text{``}\%3d\ \%5d\backslash n\text{''}, n, n * n);$$

Thus n will occupy 3 bytes, then there's a space, then n^2 in 5 bytes followed by the newline character; ten bytes in all.

Problem 2

The condition is, of course, that the value read into 'square' does not appear in any key field. To put it another way, there is no integer square root. Obviously, if top_rec and bottom_rec reach the same place without finding a match between square and key, this has happened. So the while loop becomes:

```
while (square != key) {
    skip = 10*(mid_rec - 1);
    lseek(in_cid, skip, 0);
    fscanf(in_cid, "%d %d", &sqrt, &key);
    if (bottom_rec == top_rec && square != key) {
        printf("Not found");
        exit(0);
    }
    if (key > square)
        top_rec = mid_rec - 1;
    else
        bottom_rec = mid_rec + 1;
    mid_rec = (top_rec + bottom_rec)/2;
}
```

Incidentally, notice that this is a case where the do–while construct is arguably superior to the while loop; it would save the initialisation of mid_rec and key. My reticence to use it is purely a personal phobia (although I know other C programmers who share it). I simply can't find a way of writing a do–while that *looks* nice.

I don't regard this as a weakness. You're less likely to make mistakes if you're consistent, and you're more likely to be consistent if you're comfortable with your coding style. So develop a style you like and stick to it!

Problem 3

```
search_file(filename, filesize, recsize, startbyte, numbytes, target)
char *filename;
int filesize, recsize, startbyte, numbytes, target;
{
    FILE *in_cid;
    int top_rec, bottom_rec, mid_rec, skip
    top_rec = filesize; bottom_rec = 1; key = 0;
    mid_rec = (top_rec + bottom_rec)/2;
    if ((in_cid = fopen(filename, "r")) == 0) {
        printf("No file %s", filename);
        return 0;
    }
    while (target != key) {
        skip = recsize*(mid_rec - 1);
        lseek(in_cid, skip, 0);
        fscanf(in_cid, "%s", record);
        substring(record, sub, startbyte, numbytes);
        key = atoi(sub);
        if (bottom_rec == top_rec && target != key) {
            printf("Not found");
            return 0;
        }
        if (key > target)
            top_rec = mid_rec - 1;
        else
            bottom_rec = mid_rec + 1;
        mid_rec = (top_rec + bottom_rec)/2;
    }
    return mid_rec;
}
```

The form of this function bears a remarkable resemblance to its more limited square root calculating cousin, with just a few variables replacing constants. The only significant difference is in extracting the numeric key from the current record. For simplicity, there is an assumed global character array called record into which the current record is read. A second global character array called sub also is set up, and the substring function of Chapter 6 is used to move the key field of the record into it, before it is converted to an integer for the comparisons to be made.

1. The binary search algorithm only works if, of course, the records are sorted into key order. With the squares file this was guaranteed, but now that we have a more general function who knows what the initial state of the file might be? Write a function that will sort the file into ascending order of any desired numeric keyfield.

2. Write the functions get_rec and put_rec which input from, or output to, disk the stock file structures of Chapter 13. The functions already outlined there can be modified to refer to a file rather than to an array and, together with the search and sort functions, would form the basis of a quite usable stock control system.

3. Handling files in the totally random manner I've outlined can be very time-consuming, particularly if record sizes are large. A compromise is to hold all the record key fields in main memory in record number order. Then we need search a linear array only for the target key, and the pointer to it will tell us which record number to pull from disk. Such an array is called an index. Write a function to create an index for a file, and write it to disk as another file, so that it need not be recreated as long as the file is not altered. If you want to be really flash, allow records to have multiple keys so that a file has several index files associated with it, each referring to a different key field.

CHAPTER 13

Debugging

"That is not said right," said the Caterpillar.
"Not quite *right, I'm afraid," said Alice timidly: 'some of the words*
have got altered.'
"It is wrong from beginning to end," said the Caterpillar decidedly.

Alice's Adventures in Wonderland

Whenever you write computer programs, there are two Golden Rules to bear
in mind:

Golden Rule 1. Anything that *can* go wrong, will.

Golden Rule 2. Anything that can't go wrong, probably will too. In other
words, cats miaow, dogs bark, politicians tell imaginative versions of the truth,
and programmers make mistakes.

Debugging a program can be a soul-destroying chore if it's not tackled
systematically. This is especially true of compiled programs, because they have
to be recompiled after each change. Fortunately many implementations of C
have their own debugging tools included. I'm not going to discuss such tools
here, because they vary with the implementation. Instead, I'll concentrate on
a few simple guidelines, together with some "bare hands" methods that may
be useful in the absence of fancier tools.

Common Errors

There are a number of errors that virtually everyone stating to program in C tends to make.

1. Use of $=$ *instead of* $==$. The symbol $=$ is to *assign* a value to a variable. The symbol $==$ is used to *test for equality*. So to set the variable x to the value 3 you write

$$x = 3$$

but to test this value you write

$$\text{if } (x == 3)$$
$$\ldots \text{whatever}$$

BASIC uses $=$ for both of these, so BASIC programmers have to lose this habit. Pascal programmers have to change habits completely!

Usually if you make mistakes like these you'd expect then to show up as syntax errors (with a message from the compiler to point them out). But the flexible syntax of C leads to different consequences. For example, if you write

$$\text{if } (x = 3)$$
$$\ldots \text{whatever}$$

the computer will assign the value 3 to x, then notice that $x = 3$ is true, and go on to do whatever you specified. Similarly the code

$$x == 3$$

will be evaluated as an expression (to 0 or 1) but this has no effect on the value of the variable x (or indeed on anything else).

2. Missing ;. Every statement must end with a semicolon. If the semicolon is omitted the compiler will assume that the statement continues into the next section of code, with interesting results. For example, suppose you intend to write

$$p = p + x;$$
$$q = q + y;$$

and instead write

$$p = p + x$$
$$q = q + y;$$

then the compiler will see this code as

$$p = p + xq = q + y;$$

and interpret xq as a variable name. Since this is rather unlikely as a variable name you will get the error message "undeclared variable." (If it so happens that there *is* a variable xq, worse things will happen.)

This leads to another important observation; *what the compiler sees as an error may not be the error you actually made.*

3. Missing }. This is similar, but on the level of functions rather than statements. It will usually be detected by the compiler because the number of }'s doesn't match the number of {'s. However, if you've also missed out a { or added a superfluous } elsewhere, the compiler won't notice the mistake. Your program will be unlikely to produce the results you anticipated, though.

4. Missing " ". Every string must be enclosed in quotes. If you miss them out the string will be interpreted as the name of a variable.

5. Missing */. Comments start with /* and terminate with */. If you miss out the final */ everything that follows the initial /* will be seen as a comment—including most of your program.

6. Undeclared Variables. All variables must be correctly declared. Failure to do so constitutes a syntax error and will be picked up by the compiler.

However, as remarked above, not everything seen by the compiler as an undeclared variable need correspond to a genuine undeclared variable. Other errors can lead the compiler to assume that a variable has not been declared.

Runtime Errors

The errors above are really syntax errors—breaches of the grammatical rules of the language—with the extra twist that in some cases the resulting syntax is *correct*: it just isn't what you intended! This leads us to a more serious source of error, the *runtime* error, which only shows up when the program is run. With runtime errors we've opened Pandora's box—which you'll recall was full of *bugs*—because a program with perfect syntax can still go totally haywire.

It's impossible to avoid runtime errors altogether: but you can make it easier to find them if you write structured programs that confine the problem to a clearly defined segment of code.

If a C program is well-structured, it will consist of a number of *short* functions, each standing alone as a kind of mini-program (but perhaps calling other functions). And *main* will just put them all together in a clear way. So there's a sort of tree-like hierarchy of functions, maybe a bit like this.

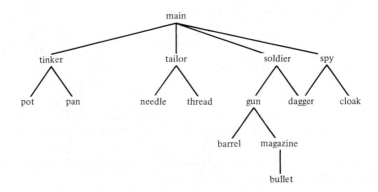

That is, *main* calls functions *tinker, tailor, soldier,* and *spy*; then *soldier* calls *gun* and *dagger*; *gun* calls *barrel* and *magazine*; and so on.

If you try to debug *main* straight away, you've got terrible problems. The bug could have burrowed its way deep into the tree; maybe way down in *magazine,* say. A sort of electronic Dutch Elm Disease. The effect of an error in *magazine* could be totally baffling by the time it propagates up to *main*.

So, of course, we should check out *magazine* first, to avoid any mistakes. In other words, we should work our way up the tree, from the twigs at the extremities (*pot, pan, needle, thread, barrel, bullet, cloak, dagger*) towards the root (*main*).

To summarize: Each (twig) function should be tested *separately,* and then the functions using tried-and-tested functions should themselves be tested, and so on. It's a matter of building on firm foundations (if twigs can be considered foundations...).

Testing a Function

The moral is: write the functions one at a time, and test each one (in a specially written test program) before using it elsewhere.

For example, here's a function that works out the volume of a box of sides a, b, c.

```
vol(a, b, c)
int a, b, c;
{
        return a*b*c;
}
```

We could test this with

```
main()
{
    int x, y, z;
    x = 2; y = 3; z = 5;
    printf("volume is %3d units", vol(x, y, z));
}
```

If you compile this and run, it will yield

volume is 30 units

and 2.3.5 is indeed 30. If skeptical, you could test again with different numbers; or use library functions to *input* lots of x, y, z values (See Chapter 8.)

If, by mistake, you'd written

```
vol(a, b, c)
int a, b, c;
{
        return a*b + c;
}
```

you'd have gotten

volume is 11 units

which would immediately show up the error. Of course this is an easy example, but it illustrates the principle.

Test Lines

Often the output demanded by the end result of a program doesn't give us enough clues about what's going on. The solution is to add temporary test lines to the program, to print out intermediate values, or whatever, to see what's happening.

Here's a (bugged) program to evaluate the yth power of an integer x.

```
power(x, y)
int x, y;
    {
        while (y > 0)
            x *= y--;
        return x;
    }
```

For a start, we need a test program to call it; say

```
main()
{
    int x, y;
    x = 7; y = 4;
    printf("power is %6d", power(x, y));
}
```

If you compile and run, you get

power is 168

which is a far cry from $7^4 = 2401$. Clearly there's something rotten in the State of Denmark, not a thousand miles away from $x *= y--$. The idea of this is to simultaneously decrement y for the *while* loop, while building up x^y by repeating multiplication. But something is amiss.

We can keep track of what's happening *inside* the loop by printing out the x and y values.

```
power(x, y)
int x, y;
    {
        while (y > 0) {
            printf("x = 3%d   y = %3d", x, y);
            x *= y--;
```

```
        }
        return x;
    }
```

This gives us an output

$x = 7$ $y = 4$ $x = 28$ $y = 3$ $x = 84$ $y = 2$ $x = 168$ $y = 1$
power is 168

The $y--$ keeps changing the y-value; so we're working out

$$7.4.3.2.1 = 168$$

by mistake.

So we replace the first two lines by

```
        power(x, y)
        int x, y;
        {
            y0 = y;
            while ...
                x *= y0; y--;
```

and discover it won't even compile! We get something like

"this variable was not in parameter list."

We forgot to *declare* the new variable $y0$. What we *should* have done was

```
        power (x, y)
        int x, y;
        {
            int y0;
            y0 = y;
            while (y > 0) {
                printf("x = %3d   y = %3d", x, y);
                x *= y0; y--;
            }
            return x;
        }
```

which give us an output

$x = 7$ $y = 4$ $x = 28$ $y = 3$ $x = 112$ $y = 2$ $x = 448$ $y = 1$
power is 1792

At this point we realize that we're repeatedly multiplying x by 4, not by 7. We've calculated

$$7.4.4.4...$$

instead of

$$7.7.7.7...$$

The way to get around this is to change

$$y0 = y;$$

to

$$y0 = x;$$

(though of course $x0$ might be a better name). Now the output is

$$x = 7 \quad y = 4 \quad x = 49 \quad y = 3 \quad x = 343 \quad y = 2 \quad x = 2401 \quad y = 1$$
$$\text{power is } 16807$$

We're multiplying by 7, all right; but we've done it once too often. 16807 is 7^5, not 7^4; and 7^4 is 2401. Any BASIC hacker will recognize the culprit immediately: we've gone around the loop once too often. So we replace

$$\text{while } (y > 0)$$

by

$$\text{while } (y > 1)$$

and this time we get

$$x = 7 \quad y = 4 \quad x = 49 \quad y = 3 \quad x = 343 \quad y = 2 \quad \text{power is } 2401$$

and all's well ... or is it?

Be Thorough

There's a hoary old tale of a tramp sitting beside a heap of twigs striking matches. Any that failed to work he threw away. Any that lit, he blew out and carefully replaced in the matchbox. When a passer-by asked why, he replied "I'm testing them to see which ones light O.K."

Programs are rather like matches. Just because they work once, that doesn't prove they'll do so on another occasion.

Test the *power* program with other values. Get it to work out 3^5, 10^3, 2^{10}, 6^1, 11^0. What do you get?

$$3^5 = 243 \qquad \text{correct}$$
$$10^3 = 1000 \qquad \text{correct}$$
$$2^{10} = 1024 \qquad \text{correct}$$
$$6^1 = 6 \qquad \text{correct}$$
$$11^0 = 11 \qquad \text{wrong (should be 1)}$$

Oops. It gets the zeroth power wrong. This is because we tell it to

$$\text{return } x;$$

at the end of the while loop. Even if it doesn't loop, x still gets returned. So we need to add a few instructions to deal separately with $y = 0$.

Problem 1

Modify *power* so that power $(x, 0)$ is always 1, as it should be.

Problem 2

An efficient way to deal with test lines is to write a function called *debug* which prints out the current value of a given variable, along with a message to identify which one it is. It should have two arguments, *message* and *value*. For example, if the variable x has the value 99 then the statement

$$debug("x =", x);$$

should produce the output

$$>> x = 99$$

(where the $>>$ is to distinguish the debugging message from anything else that the program prints out).
   Write such a function.

Problem 3

Improve the function from Problem 2 as follows. Set up a global array called _count (the initial underline is there to make sure it's not one of the arrays already in the program) which, for each variable, counts how many times that variable is called by *debug*. Modify *debug* to take three arguments: *message*, *value*, and *refno*. The new variable *refno* gives the relevant element of the array. The output should look something like this.

$$>> \text{Reference Number } 2: x = 99: \text{count} = 5$$

Dormant Bugs

How do we prove conclusively that a program does precisely what it was written to do? I don't want to get involved in too complicated a philosophical discussion (because that's where we are headed) but, broadly it's a bit like asking an astronomer whether the sun will rise tomorrow. If he is very pedantic he might answer that the earth has been going around the sun for a long time now and we have a body of physical laws which suggest that it will continue to do so in a regular way, and that the smart money would be on this continuing to be the case tomorrow; but he would add that he has no way of knowing whether our physical laws are right and that what we have observed for thousands of years might in fact be a manifestation of a much more complex law whose effect, tomorrow, might be to reverse the direction of the earth's rotation or to take it out of orbit completely.
   By analogy, because a program behaves correctly for the first thousand sets of data input to it, there's no absolute guarantee that it will work for the thousand and first. In fact, bugs often don't become apparent until months or

even years after a program has been apparently successfully completed and has been run without problems dozens or even hundreds of times. This isn't really surprising; after all, it's the conditions that occur least often that the programmer is most likely to overlook.

Here's an example. We are writing a suite of programs for the Nether Hopping Electricity Board to handle its customer accounts. They explain to us that there are two tariffs, A and B. On the A tariff the consumer pays a quarterly standing charge of $15 and then pays for units used at a rate of 4¢ per unit. On the B tariff the consumer pays no standing charge and pays 7¢ per unit. So we write a function:

```
bill(units, tariff)
int units;
char tariff;
{
    if (tariff == 'A')
            return (15 + 4*units/100);
    else
            return (7*units/100);
}
```

and a main program rather like

```
main()
{
    int units;
    char tariff;
    units = 1035
    tariff = 'B';
    printf("Fred Bloggs % 6d", bill(units, tariff));
}
```

O.K. I know that in practice we'd input the 1035 and the "B," along with the customer's name (Fred Bloggs) and no doubt the address, account number, credit rating, and shirt size. But you get the idea.

So we test this piece of code and it works fine and we go away muttering that it is a waste of our remarkable talents to be given Noddy programs like this to write.

And it does work fine for years, and then one day it prints a bill for $0.00. Of course, nobody notices because it's one of thousands of bills and anyway it's probably enveloped automatically. The recipient is puzzled and probably amused by the bill because it shows how stupid computers are but there seems no point in taking any action so he throws the bill away. Unfortunately, we wrote another program in the same suite which stores the date when each bill was dispatched and if it does not receive confirmation that the bill has been paid within 28 days, it prints a final demand notice. This time the recipient is more irritated than amused but just consigns it to the waste paper basket, as before. At this point things start to go seriously wrong. The routine that checks the delay between presentation of the account and payment issues an order to the maintenance department to cut off any consumer who still hasn't paid after 60 days.

What's happened? Easy! The consumer is an old-age pensioner who has taken advantage of one of the long winter break packages that the travel companies offer to senior citizens. He was out of the country for just over three months and used no electricity in a full account period. He is also an unusually frugal user of electricity so he's on tariff B. That's why the system printed out a request for zero payment, and of course it won't happen very often because very few people will be away from home for that long, and tariff B users are likely to be thin on the ground, too. For the problem to occur, the consumer has to fit both conditions.

Once seen, the bug is easily squashed, just add to *main* a line:

```
if (bill(units, tariff) == 0)
    printf("send no bill");
```

so that the system is warned against the offending action.

This problem is supposed to have occurred in an early computer system, although whether it's a folk tale I wouldn't like to say. In any event, I think it illustrates neatly how a bug can lie dormant almost indefinitely.

The moral is: when you invent data to test a program, don't do so at random. Choose values at and close to branch values in the program. If a statement says:

```
if (u < 30) {
    do something or other
}
```

then run a test with u at 29.9999; and 30; and another at 30.0001. You may have meant:

```
if (u <= 30) {
    do something or other
}
```

If you test only at $u = 15$ and $u = 160$ you won't notice the error.

Make sure test data have been chosen so that every section of the program is executed at some time. And of course make sure you know exactly what the answer should be for each set of test data.

Answers

Problem 1

```
power(x, y)
int x, y;
```

```
{
    if (y == 0)
        return 1;
    else {
        int y0;
        y0 = x;
        while (y > 1) {
            x *= y0; y--;
        }
        return x;
    }
}
```

Problem 2

```
debug(message, value)
{
    char *message;
    int value;
    printf(">>%s %d", message, value);
}
```

Problem 3

```
int _count[];
debug(message, value, refno)
{
    char *message;
    int value, refno;
    printf("Reference number %d:%s%d", refno, message, value);
}
```

Note: In Problems 1 and 2 we have, for simplicity, assumed that the variables under consideration are of type int. See Project 2 below.

PROJECTS

1. It would be useful, in connection with the "debug" function, to be able to remove the test lines automatically once the program has been fully debugged. Write a function **dedebug** that reads the program from a file, removes all **debug** statements, and writes it back to the file.

2. Modify the answers to Problems 2 and 3, so that no assumptions are made about the type of the variable whose value is printed out.

CHAPTER 14

Rational Arithmetic

"What day of the month is it?" he said, turning to Alice: he had taken his watch out of his pocket, and was looking at it uneasily, shaking it every now and then, and holding it to his ear.

Alice considered a little, and then said, "the fourth".

"Two days wrong!" sighed the Hatter. "I told you butter wouldn't suit the works!" he added, looking angrily at the March Hare.

"It was the best butter," the March Hare meekly replied.

Alice's Adventures in Wonderland

Most modern high-level languages offer you a choice of integers or floating point arithmetic. Generally, so far as the programmer is concerned, that choice is dictated by the kinds of numbers he or she wants to play with; if you want fractional values, you've got to use float.

However, there are other factors to consider. On the assumption that your computer doesn't deal with floating point calculations in hardware (and unless you're very rich it won't—math coprocessors for current 16-bit machines add at least $500 to the cost of the machine, and you can't get them at all for vanilla flavored 8-bit systems) it is going to do such sums in a fairly leisurely manner. This is so because floating point arithmetic algorithms are quite complex animals. I don't want to get involved in the gory details, but just to get the flavor of the problem, think about the following sum

$$5.83 + 642.1$$

In a *decimal* floating point system, these numbers could be seen as

| 1 | 583000 | that is the '1' and '3' indicate the positions of the |
| 3 | 642100 | decimal points from the left hand ends of the numbers |

To perform the addition, the points must be aligned effectively. This is equivalent to bumping the '1' by two and shifting right its corresponding number twice.

3   005830

3   642100

Now we can add the two numbers, leaving the '3' alone.

3   647930

That's equivalent to 647.93, which is correct.

So a simple addition has turned into a loop of shifts and increments followed by an addition. If the number was represented in 24 bits we could need to perform the loop (shift-increment-test) 24 times before doing the addition. In practice, there are several technical problems that make the algorithm still more complicated.

Fixing the Problem

So it appears that you can't have high-speed arithmetic and fractions. But floating point provides not only a representation for fractions, but a colossal range of representable number. On any home micro you can happily work with numbers as large as:

100,000,000,000,000,000,000,000,000,000,000,000

But, be honest, how many times have you actually needed anything remotely like that number?

Perhaps, then, there's a compromise; a representation that will allow fractions and execute arithmetic relatively fast, but won't let you talk about the distances between star systems.

Well, there are several. You can, for example, simply fix a point at an arbitrary position in a word and then perform all calculations on the basis that all numbers are represented in this form. This "fixed point" representation was common on early computers but is pretty much extinct now.

A more promising alternative was proposed by Berthold Horn (see "Software Practice and Experience," Volume 8, Number 2). His scheme goes like this: See a number as a pair of integers whose value is one of them divided by the other. Thus 3.2 appears as 32/10 or possibly 16/5. In general, let's talk about a number A as the pair (a, a') whose value is a/a'. It's obvious where the term "rational arithmetic" comes from; each number is a ratio of integers.

We can look at some of the implications of adopting this strategy by examining the general algebraic results for the four basic operations on two numbers, A and B:

i) Addition

$$A + B = a/a' + b/b'$$

$$= (ab' + a'b)/(a'b')$$

This result is another ratio, so that if $R = A + B$, $r = ab' + a'b$ and $r' = ab'$. That's pretty convenient, but there is a fly in the ointment. Clearly the multiples (ab' etc.) require double length words. But r and r' must be returned to single words. So there are going to be problems concerned with avoiding overflow. We could minimise these difficulties by using a lowest common multiple algorithm, but that would be rather time-consuming and, in view of our general aim here, self-defeating.

ii) Subtraction

$$A - B = a/a' - b/b'$$

$$= a/a' + (-b)/b'$$

It's only necessary to form the two's complement of b and then call the addition function. No new problems here.

iii) Multiplication

$$AB = a/a' \times b/b'$$

$$= (a \times b)/(a' \times b')$$

Again, the rational result has a convenient form ($r = a \times b, r' = a' \times b'$) and, also as before, we're going to get overflow problems.

iv) Division

$$A/B = (a/a')/(b/b')$$

$$= (a \times b')/(a' \times b)$$

No problem with this. On the contrary, a pleasant surprise. Division algorithms are usually complex, slow, or both and, in any event, a real pain. This one is trivial.

On the whole, this is looking pretty quick. Multiplication and division each require only two integer multiply operations, and addition and subtraction need three followed by an addition.

Overflow

We had better confront the overflow problem before getting too complacent. To get a grasp of the difficulties we'll examine what would happen in a system in which we chose two 6-bit fields to form our numbers. Thus 3.1 and 1.8 could appear as:

$$
\begin{array}{lcc}
 & 31 & 10 \\
3.1 & 011111 & 001010 \\
 & 18 & 10 \\
1.8 & 010010 & 001010 \\
\end{array}
$$

Adding these two numbers using the raw algorithm gives:

$$31 \times 10 + 18 \times 10 \quad : \quad 000\overline{111101}010$$
$$10 \times 10 \quad : \quad 000001100100$$

While the result remains in 12-bit fields, it is, of course, exactly right (490/100). However, we have the problem of crunching the data back into 6 bits. A fairly obvious technique is to shift both words left until one of them has two different senior digits (i.e., all leading non-significant digits have been lost). Then extract the senior 6 bits from each, thus:

$$
\begin{array}{ll}
011110 & = 30 \\
000110 & = 6 \\
\end{array}
$$

This gives the result 5. At one level, it isn't too surprising that we're getting errors in the first decimal place, because we can't get 100 into the 6-bit denominator and we clearly need it for 2 decimal places.

However, if we consider the result a little more carefully there are two distinct oddities. First, since the denominators happened to be the same, there was no need to use the general algorithm at all—we could simply have added the two numerators. This would have given an exact answer and saved time into the bargain. So it would seem to be worthwhile testing for this condition. Second we could have "cancelled" the second number from 18/10 to 9/5. If you repeat the sum having done so, you get

$$
\begin{array}{ll}
0000\overline{111101}01 & (= 245) \\
000000110010 & (= 50) \\
\end{array}
$$

Selecting the 6 most significant bits gives exactly the same result as before! A little thought indicates that the bit patterns are (and must be) unchanged except for a shift right in each case.

But won't the $ab' + a'b$ expression exceed 12 bits if its terms are large enough? Actually, no. In 6 bits the maximum value is 011111, or 1F hex. So the expression can only reach $2 \times 1F \times 1F = 782 = 011110000010$, comfortably below the 12-bit limit. There *would* be a problem at the other end of the scale if all the terms were negative, but they can't be, because a' and b' are always positive divisions, sign being indicated by a and b.

It's easy to show algebraically that overflow is impossible for any word size. If you're still suspicious, I leave it to you as an exercise.

A Practical Organization

Having convinced ourselves that this scheme ought to work in principle, let's turn our attention to a specific implementation. We could choose to represent each part of the rational number (i.e., the divisor and the dividend) in an int, and declare a new type, rat:

$$\begin{aligned}
&\text{typedef struct } \{ \\
&\qquad \text{int top;} \\
&\qquad \text{int bottom;} \\
&\} \text{ rat;}
\end{aligned}$$

(i.e., a 'rat' has the form top/bottom). Now we'll be able to declare rational numbers, and pointers to them, as for instance

$$\text{rat } n, *p;$$
$$p = \&n;$$

which is just like an ordinary variable definition.

The range of numbers that are representable in this form clearly depends on the size of an int. If it is 16 bits then this range is -32768 to 32767, just as it would be for integers, because to achieve these extremes we clearly need the smallest possible denominator (1). Equally clearly, we can represent nothing closer to zero than 0.00003052 (1/32767). We should be able to expect a precision of 4 significant figures. This is perfectly adequate for many purposes (lots of us got along with 4 figure logs for years) but with a modern 32 bit micro a range of ± 2 billion is achievable, with a precision of around 9 significant figures. That's better accuracy than some floating point systems and, while it lacks their range, it's hardly restrictive. We shall find, however, that things are not quite as rosy as they might at first sight appear.

Functions

What functions will go to make up the package? Obviously the four arithmetic operations already discussed; but we also need mechanisms for getting numbers from the outside world into rational format and vice versa. The simplest technique here is going to be to write functions that convert between strings and rational format, much as atoi converts between a string and an integer.

Because a rat is a structure, we can only pass pointers as arguments, and that means that a pointer to the result must appear in the argument list. This leaves the possibility of returning something else. The *sign* of the result seems like a sensible contender for this honor. So we'll standardise on the following:

If p, q and r are pointers to rats

add (p, q, r)	gives	$*r = *p + *q$
sub (p, q, r)	gives	$*r = *p - *q$
mpy (p, q, r)	gives	$*r = *p \times *q$
div (p, q, r)	gives	$*r = *p/*q$

In each of the above cases, if the value pointed to by r is negative, -1 is returned, if zero, zero is returned, and if positive $+1$ is returned. The conversion functions are:

> ator(p, r)   which converts a string pointed to by p to a rat
> pointed to by r.

and

> rtoa(r, p)   which converts a rat pointed to by r to a string
> pointed to by p.

Double or Nothing

Before leaping into action and writing some code, there's one remaining potential fly in the ointment to consider. It concerns the intermediate double length results that are generated by terms like ab'.

These are easy to deal with if, and only if, your compiler implements the long int type *and* it is a double length integer. It would be nice to make the package more generally applicable than that; that is, to make it more portable.

Let's set our signts rather lower than total portability for a moment and think about a specific and rather common case: that in which ints are 16 bits, chars are 8 bits and longs are either not implemented or are also 16 bits. If we simply multiply two ints together, the result is actually the low order 16 bits of the true answer; useless for our purpose. However, suppose we see the numbers in their constituent bytes:

$$A \quad ahigh \quad alow$$
$$B \quad bhigh \quad blow$$

and treat the sum as a long multiplication, base 256. If the result appears in 4 bytes $c0, c1, c2, c3$ then the values can be seen like this:

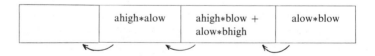

	ahigh*alow	ahigh*blow + alow*bhigh	alow*blow

The carry problem is now very easily handled. Simply use integers to hold the intermediate results and, having extracted the low order 8 bits with a mask, shift right 8 bits to look at the carry.

We could write a function on this basis called long_mpy, which takes two ints a and b, multiplies them together and leaves the result in a char array pointed to by c.

```
long_mpy(a, b, c)
int a, b;
char *c;
{
      char temp1[4], temp2[4];
```

```
int temp, alow, ahigh, blow, bhigh, sign = 1;
if (a < 0) {
    sign *= -1;
    a *= -1;
}
if (b < 0) {
    sign *= -1;
    b *= -1;
}
alow = a; blow = b;
ahigh = a >> 8; bhigh = b >> 8;
temp = alow * blow;
temp1[0] = temp;
temp1[1] = temp >> 8;
temp1[2] = temp1[3] = 0;
temp = ahigh * blow;
temp2[0] = temp2[3] = 0;
temp2[1] = temp;
temp2[2] = temp >> 8;
long_add(temp1, temp2, c);
temp = alow * bhigh;
temp1[0] = temp1[3] = 0;
temp1[1] = temp;
temp1[2] = temp >> 8;
long_add(temp1, c, c);
temp = ahigh * bhigh;
temp1[0] = temp1[1] = 0;
temp1[2] = temp;
temp1[3] = temp >> 8;
long_add(temp1, c, c)
if (sign < 0)
    negate(c);
}
```

This function assumes that a and b are positive. If not we just make them positive and keep a record of the sign. After that, it's just a question of forming the terms of the result in 4-byte arrays and adding them together. I'm using a new routine called long_add for this, because we're going to need it anyway when dealing with additions. Finally, we need to recreate the correct sign, by calling a routine called negate if necessary.

Negate just flips the bits of the 4 bytes passed to it and then uses long_add to add 1 to the result:

```
negate(n)
char n[];
{
```

```
            int i;
            char one[4];
            one[0] = 1; one[1] = one[2] = one[3] = 0;
            for (i = 0; i < 4; i++)
                n[i] = ~n[i];
            long_add(n, one, n);
        }
```

long_add uses to new techniques:

```
            long_add(a, b, c)
            char a[ ], b[ ], c[ ];
            {
                unsigned temp = 0;
                int i;
                for (i = 0; i < 4; i++) {
                    temp >>= 8;
                    temp = temp + a[i] + b[i];
                    c[i] = temp;
                }
            }
```

There's one further function that tinkers with these 4-byte arrays, the one that takes the double length numerators and denominators and recreates a standard rat structure from them. Assuming that n is a pointer to the numerator array, d is a pointer to the denominator array, and r is a pointer to the target rat structure, we get:

```
            dtor(n, d, r)
            char *n, *d;
            rat *r;
            {
                while (highbit(n + 3) ∧ nextbit(n + 3) == 0
                        && highbit(d + 3) ∧ nextbit(d + 3) == 0) {
                    left(n);
                    left(d);
                }
                r -> top = *(n + 3) << 8 + *(n + 2);
                r -> bottom = *(d + 3) << 8 + *(d + 2);
            }
```

This is straightforward enough. We compare the two senior bits of the numerator and perform the same function for the denominator. While they are the same in each case we shift both of them left one bit. As soon as either has different bits in the two senior positions, there are no more insignificant leading digits, so we transfer the high order 16 bits of the numerator and denominator to the top and bottom respectively of the fraction.

That leaves highbit, nextbit and left to write

```
highbit(c)
char *c;
{
        return(*c & 0x80 ? 1 : 0);
}
```

Thus highbit returns 1 or 0 depending on whether the senior bit of the array was 1 or 0.

Similarly nextbit returns 1 or 0 depending on whether the next most senior bit is 1 or 0:

```
nextbit(c)
char *c;
{
        return(*c & 0x40 ? 1 : 0);
}
```

Now for left:

```
left(c)
char *c;
{
        int i;
        c += 3;
        for (i = 0; i < 4; i++) {
                *c <<= 1;
                if (i == 3)
                        break;
                *c += highbit(c - 1);
                c--;
        }
}
```

Obviously, the basic technique is to shift the high order byte (i.e., that pointed to by $c + 3$) left, thus leaving room for a possible carry on the right. Then use highbit on the next byte to add in the carry. This process is repeated 4 times, *except* that on the last repetition we don't want a carry drawn in from next byte. Hence the "if($i == 3$) break;".

Portability Considerations

The reason I have separated these functions out and examined them before the main rational suite is that they are clearly nonportable. It wouldn't be difficult to make them handle N-byte arrays, with each byte containing B bits and then allow N and B to be the subject of #define statements, but it is questionable whether this is worthwhile. After all, it may not be sensible to employ such a structure at all if, for instance, long ints are implemented as

double length ints. In any case, generalization will probably be at the expense
of speed and we should bear in mind that it is fast execution that provides
the *raison d'etre* for this whole exercise. So it's more sensible to require
the implementor to provide equivalents to these functions for the target
configuration, and give him or her the rest of the source code. Speaking of
which ...

```
add(p, q, r)
rat *p, *q, *r;
{
        char m1[4], m2[4], m3[4], m4[4];
        long_mpy(p —> top, q —> bottom, m1);
        long_mpy(p —> bottom, q —> top, m2);
        long_mpy(p —> bottom, q —> bottom, m3);
        long_add(m1, m2, m4);
        dtor(m4, m3, r);
        return (r —> top ? r —> top/abs(r —> top) : 0);
}
```

This is a fairly unremarkable implementation of the original algorithm,
except for the mechanism which returns the sign of the result (as -1, 0 or 1
for negative, zero or positive, you'll recall). The idea is that the numerator is
tested for non-zero. If it isn't then zero is returned, but if it is, the numerator
is divided by the positive version of itself. Of course, that will produce either
1 or -1, depending on its original sign. The denominator does not affect
things since it's always positive.

Lies, Damned Lies and Computer Programs

Or is it? I claimed it was at the beginning of this chapter because we can ensure
that ator keeps it that way, and add forms the new denominator only from
the old ones. So does sub and mpy. But div puts a spanner in the works. It
forms the new denominator from a numerator times a denominator, and the
numerator could be negative. All is not lost, though. We simply need to modify
dtor to test for a negative denominator, and change the sign of both top and
bottom if it finds one.

Problem 1

Make the necessary changes to dtor.

Subtraction

This one's a doddle:

```
sub(p, q, r)
rat *p, *q, *r;
```

```
{
        rat copy;
        copy.top = -(q -> top);
        copy.bottom = q -> bottom;
        return add(p, &copy, r);
}
```

The numerator of the subtrahend is just negated and add is called. However, note that we have to make a local copy of this value, otherwise the data given to the function will be altered. This problem only arises, of course, when pointers, rather than actual data are passed.

Also note that we want to return what add returns.

Multiplication

This is perfectly straightforward:

```
mpy(p, q, r)
rat *p, *q, *r;
{
        char *m1, *m2;
        long_mpy(p -> top, q -> top, m1);
        long_mpy(p -> bottom, q -> bottom, m2);
        dtor(m1, m2, r);
        return (r -> top : r -> top/abs(r -> top)?0);
}
```

Division

No problems here either:

```
div(p, q, r)
rat p, q, r;
{
        char *m1, *m2;
        long_mpy(p -> top, q -> bottom, m1);
        long_mpy(p -> bottom, q -> top, m2);
        dtor(m1, m2, r);
        return (r -> top : r -> top/abs(r -> top)?0);
}
```

The Conversion Routines

That just leaves us with the problem of communicating with the outside world. Here's a possible ator:

```
ator(p, r)
char *p;
rat *r;
{
        char copy[10], *pc, *s;
        strcpy(copy, p);
        r –> bottom = 1;
        pc = copy;
        s = pc + strlen(pc) – 1;
        while (*s != '.') {
                r –> bottom *= 10;
                s––;
        }
        *s = '\0';
        strcat(copy, s + 1);
        r –> top = atoi(copy);
}
```

It works like this. A local copy of the string is made so that it can be messed about with impunity. The denominator is set to 1, and a pointer (s) to the end of the string. Then we move back through the string, looking for the point, and multiplying the denominator repeatedly by 10 until we find it. Finally, we concatenate the string after the point on to the string before the point to create an integer which can be passed to atoi and thus used to generate the numerator.

Obviously, the string must contain a point for this to work, and the number of digits in the string must not exceed 5 (in fact, it mustn't be bigger than 32767).

The rtoa routine does little more than a glorified long division:

```
rtoa(r, p)
rat *r;
char *p;
{
        rat copy;
        int dp;
        *p = ' ';
        copy.top = r –> top;
        copy.bottom = r –> bottom;
        if (copy.top < 0) {
                copy.top = –copy.top;
                *p = '–';
        }
        sprintf(p + 1, "%5d.", copy.top/copy.bottom);
        copy.top %= copy.bottom;
        p = p + strlen(p);
```

```
for (dp = 1; dp < 5; dp++) {
    while (copy.top > 3276) {
        copy.top >>= 1;
        copy.bottom >>= 1;
    }
    copy.top *= 10;
    sprintf(p, "%1d", copy.top/copy.bottom);
    p++;
    copy.top %= copy.bottom;
}
}
```

First, a copy of the rat is made and is forced to positive. A space or minus sign is placed at the beginning of the output string as appropriate. The integer digits follow this by performing an integer divide into the string using sprintf. A point is located in the string in the same operation. Then, taking the remainder, we simply repeat the divide operation after first multiplying the top by 10 to get the next decimal place. Unfortunately, top*10 can overflow; the rather mysterious little while loop ensures that doesn't happen by repeatedly dividing top and bottom by 2 until the top is less than 32767/10.

And Now the Bad News....

Try the package out. You'll find that it behaves much as predicted most of the time. However there are odd occasions on which it suddenly starts producing wildly inaccurate answers.

Problem 2

See if you can run down the nature of the bug. (Hint: it isn't *exactly* bug.) Perhaps you can think of ways of fixing it.

Answers

Problem 1

This is pretty run-of-the-mill. First test the sign of d with a call to highbit. Then, if it's ngeative, call negate on both n and d. This can be done anywhere before the data are transferred to the rat pointed to by r, but if it's done at the beginning of the routine the while condition can be simplified, because we then know that the highbit of d may not be 1:

```
dtor(n, d, r)
char *n, *d;
rat *r;
{
```

```
        if (highbit(d + 3)) {
              negate(d);
              negate(n);
        }
        while (highbit(n + 3) ∧ nextbit(n + 3) == 0 && !(highbit(d + 3))) {
              left(n);
              left(d)
        }
        r -> top = *(n + 3) << 8 + *(n + 2);
        r -> bottom = *(d + 3) << 8 + *(d + 2);
}
```

Problem 2

The way to tackle this is to look at the intermediate results in rational form, and also at the 4 byte arrays. You can just include a few printfs such as:

  printf("top of r: %x bottom of r: %x\n", r -> top, r -> bottom); It's convenient to keep the output in hex because that makes it easy to see how the binary patterns are shifting around. What you will find is that the 32-bit results are behaving exactly as they should and that the rationals are being formed correctly from them. You also should notice that the major inaccuracies are occuring only when the denominator is small. Once you've seen this the reason is fairly obvious. If there are, say, 10 significant bits in the denominator, the integer held is of the order of 1000, so the accuracy is about 0.1%. On the other hand, with five significant bits, the value is around 30 and the accuracy has worsened catastrophically to around 3%.

PROJECTS

What can be done about this? Here are a few suggestions:

1. Double the size of the representations. This is going to be fairly easy if you have a processor (such as a Motorola 68000) which has 32-bit registers and can therefore perform the necessary arithmetic directly. Otherwise, the extra coding is going to slow things down rather a lot.

2. Allow the elements of a rat to maintain accuracy *not* by truncating them below 16 significant bits, but rather by keeping a record of the effective point position in each case, and tidying up the result as late as possible. This is getting uncomfortably close to a conventional floating point format, though.

3. Instead of performing a dtor conversion at the end of each operation, convert directly to alpha (i.e., write dtoa). This will preserve accuracy quite nicely but it leaves the problem of doing base 256 long divisions. That's likely to be messy *and* slow.

4. Try to devise a "normalization" process by which the rationals themselves are kept close to unity, the area where errors will be at a minimum. Again, you'll need an extra field to hold multipying factors.

Postscript

I have tried to present the material in this chapter much as I conceived it, warts and all. Thus where I originally made an error at the design stage (for instance, in assuming the denominator would always be positive) I've left it in, until the point where I discovered the error of my ways.

By doing so, I hope to have shown up the power of a modular approach to software design. Because I already had the functions highbit and negate, and because the problem could be localized to dtor, the solution to this particular incorrect problem specification was trivial. It would not have been so easy if the code had been written inline.

Of course, if analysts and programmers didn't make mistakes it wouldn't matter much. But they do; experience may make them better, but never perfect. So it's important to look at the *ways* in which errors can occur and consider damage limitation techniques. In my view, textbook writers often are too ready to present their final, immaculate algorithms and code, and to sweep under the carpet the false starts and rewrites that go into the body of the iceberg (if I may mix my metaphors).

CHAPTER 15

Implementing Turtle Graphics...

"Once," said the Mock Turtle at last, with a deep sigh," I was a real *Turtle."*

Alice's Adventures in Wonderland

Turtle Graphics were invented by Seymour Papert in the 1960's and form the best known part of his introductory programming language, Logo. The idea is that lines can be drawn on the screen by an (imaginary) turtle which happens to be carrying a pen around with it. It can be commanded to head off in any given direction, travel a specific distance, lower the pen so that it leaves a track as it goes, or raise it so that no trace is left. In some implementations the turtle is a robot, and the name is more appropriate, but the side effects on carpets can be undesirable.

The turtle uses no conventional Cartesian or Polar coordinate system explicitly, but rather an implicit mixture of both. This makes it especially useful for young children; but it has deservedly gained widespread popularity elsewhere.

Here, I'm going to examine in detail a turtle graphics package which uses only integer arithmetic, on the grounds that several popular C compilers support high resolution graphics but not float. Later we'll look briefly at how it could be revised to give somewhat improved accuracy using float.

Turning Turtle

We're going to implement the following primitive operations:

penup   Lift the pen, so that the turtle can move without leaving a trace.
pendown   Lower the pen again.
turn   Turn the turtle through a specified number of degrees anti-clockwise.
turnto   Set the turtle heading to an absolute angle measured anticlock-wise from a reference line at 3 o'clock.
position Set the turtle down at a specified position, expressed in Cartesian coordinate terms.
move   Move the turtle a specified distance on its current heading.

So the sequence of commands:

position(50, 20);
pendown();
turnto(30);
move(25);
turn(60);
move(20);

will have the effects shown in Figure 15.1. Incidentally, the function names

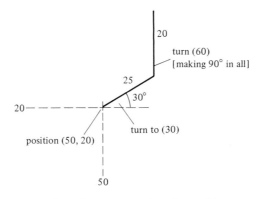

FIGURE 15.1. Effect of a sequence of turtle graphics commands.

I've chosen are not those of "standard" Logo. This is easily justified, firstly because there *is* no standard, and secondly because I want to minimize the number of primitives. Most Logos have the primitives LEFT and RIGHT which have exactly the same significance as our 'turn'. Thus the form LEFT 30 is the same as turn(30) and RIGHT 60 is equivalent to turn(-60).

Anyway, you can see that, if we can implement these functions, we will have a powerful graphics tool.

But First, The Snags....

A typical medium resolution display on a microcomputer is about 250×200 pixels, maybe a bit better, maybe less. On the other hand, as I said in Chapter 6, a C integer variable is often held in a 16-bit word, giving a range of -32768 to 32767. The screen coordinates just about fit into an 8-bit field, so we've got about double the precision available that we need. The trick is to make this work for us.

Suppose we store the turtle coordinates 256 times larger than their true values. If the centre of the display is seen as $(0, 0)$ and coordinates range from -125 to $+125$, we'll be storing values in the range -32000 to $+32000$, comfortably inside the integer range. Only when a point is plotted do we need to deal with the true values, and those are simply the stored values shifted right eight bits.

In effect, we have better than two decimal places of accuracy. This will help to control round-off errors.

As we shall see, all references to sine and cosine will also be multiplied by 256, so that we can obtain integer approximations to these functions that also will give us an effective 2 decimal places. So here's the basic idea:

1. Store all point coordinates 256 times too big.
2. Hold distances in their true form (i.e., *not* times 256).
3. Evaluate (integer part of $256 * \sin A$) rather than $\sin A$ (and similarly for $\cos A$).

Triggery—Pokery

That leaves the most pressing problem of how to deal with item 3. The simplest (though rather inelegant) solution is to hold an array of all the necessary sine values for all integer angles from $0°$ to $90°$. We'll examine this first, and worry about neater solutions later. Table 15.1 shows the values we need.

It's clear that all functions will need access to this information, so we need a global array. While we're thinking about global variables it's also evident that several functions will need to know where the turtle is, which way it's headed, and whether it's writing at the moment. So we have

int s[91], x_turtle, y_turtle, heading, writing;

TABLE 15.1. 256 × sin A (rounded to the nearest integer)

angle A	sin(A)*256	angle A	sin(A)*256	angle A	sin(A)*256
0	0	30	128	60	222
1	4	31	132	61	224
2	9	32	136	62	226
3	13	33	139	63	228
4	18	34	143	64	230
5	22	35	147	65	232
6	27	36	150	66	234
7	31	37	154	67	236
8	36	38	158	68	237
9	40	39	161	69	239
10	44	40	165	70	241
11	49	41	168	71	242
12	53	42	171	72	243
13	58	43	175	73	245
14	62	44	178	74	246
15	66	45	181	75	247
16	71	46	184	76	248
17	75	47	187	77	249
18	79	48	190	78	250
19	83	49	193	79	251
20	88	50	196	80	252
21	92	51	199	81	253
22	96	52	202	82	254
23	100	53	204	83	254
24	104	54	207	84	255
25	108	55	210	85	255
26	112	56	212	86	255
27	116	57	215	87	256
28	120	58	217	88	256
29	124	59	219	89	256

s is our sine array, x_turtle and y_turtle give the turtle's current Cartesian coordinates, heading gives its current angle to the reference line and writing is a flag which is set to 1 if the pen is down and 0 if it is up.

We'll need a function, initialize, which sets the turtle to the centre of the screen, a heading of 0° and the pendown state. It also can set up s. Obviously, s *could* be initialized by writing a laborious sequence of statements such as:

$$s[0] = 0;$$
$$\vdots$$
$$s[91] = 256;$$

91 times, or, if your compiler supports initializers:

$$\text{int } s[91] = \{0, \ldots\ldots$$
$$\ldots, 256\};$$

Perhaps we can do better. No doubt you have a BASIC interpreter on your machine. Use it to set up a file of the values we want like this, say:

```
10  CREATE # 10, "isin.dat"
20  FOR angle = 0 to 90
30  PRINT # 10, INT (256 * SIN (angle * 3.142 / 180) + 0.5)
40  NEXT angle
50  CLOSE*10
```

(Note the 0.5 in line 30 to provide the correct round-off.)

Now we can read this back into s inside initialize:

```
initialize()
{
        FILE *cid;
        int angle;
        heading = 0;
        pendown();
        position(XCENTRE, YCENTRE);
        cid = fopen("isin.dat", "r");
        for (angle = 0; angle < 91; angle++)
                fscanf(cid, "%d", &s[angle]);
        fclose(cid);

}
```

First, the heading is set to zero and the pen placed down. The turtle is positioned in the centre of the screen. Where exactly this is depends on your system, of course, so I've left it open. XCENTRE and YCENTRE can be the subject of suitable # define statements. Finally, the file of values created by BASIC is read back into s.

Next the trig functions:

```
isin(a)
int a;
{
        if (a <= 90)
                return s[a];
        if (a <= 180)
                return s[180 − a];
        if (a <= 270)
                return −s[a − 180];
        if (a > 270)
                return −s[360 − a];
}
icos(a)
int a;
{
        a = 90 − a;
```

```
if (a < 0)
    a += 360;
return isin(a);
}
```

Here the '*i*' prefix is just to remind us that we're doing *integer* trig (and getting numbers 256 times as large as the usual sin and cos). I've assumed a lies in the range $0°$ to $360°$ in both functions, so the 'turn' function will have to ensure this is the case.

The Turtle Commands

That's dealt with the housekeeping; now we can turn our attention to the turtle commands proper.

```
turn(a)
int a;
{
    heading += a;
    heading %= 360;
    if (heading < 0)
        heading += 360;
}
```

First, heading is incremented by the angle *a* and the result evaluated modulo 360. It might seem that this is as far as we need to go, but in fact there's an extra problem.

Let's examine a couple of examples to see the difficulty. Suppose that heading initially evaluates to 370. The mod operation will generate 10, which is correct. However, if heading were -370 to start with, the % operation gives -10, which is not inside the required range. In mathematical terms, the result of a mod operation here *should* be 350, which is, of course, equivalent to -10 and fulfills our conditions.

The problem is that the % operator is not strictly a modulus operator. It evaluates the *remainder* of the division, which is clearly not necessarily positive. So we need to add 360 to any negative result to stay within range.

Having spotted this trick, turnto is trivial.

```
turnto(a)
int a;
{
    heading = a % 360;
    if (heading < 0)
        heading += 360;
}
```

The pen movement commands simply alter the state of writing

```
                    pendown()
                    {
                            writing = 1;
                    }
                    penup()
                    {
                            writing = 0;
                    }
```

The move function is a little more complicated.

```
            move(dist)
            int dist;
            {
                    int x, y;
                    x = x_turtle + dist*icos(heading);
                    y = y_turtle + dist*isin(heading);
                    if (writing)
                            line(x_turtle >> 8, y_turtle >> 8, x >> 8, y >> 8);
                    x_turtle = x;
                    y_turtle = y;
            }
```

Think about the basic relationships here (ignoring our 256 fiddle factor):

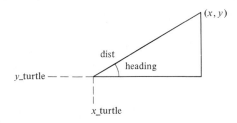

We have

$$x - x\_turtle = dist * \cos(heading)$$

and

$$y - y\_turtle = dist * \sin(heading)$$

If we insert our icos and isin values, the right hand sides of these equations are multiplied by 256. To compensate, x, y, x_turtle and y_turtle are also multiplied by 256, but, of course, nothing needs to happen to dist.

Thus the new values of x and y are evaluated and, if the turtle should be writing at the moment, a line is drawn. The precise form of this function call obviously depends on your graphics library. I'm assuming that there is a function

$$\text{line}(a, b, c, d);$$

that will draw a line from (a, b) to (c, d). Notice that the arguments are all right shifted 8 bits to divide out the 256. Finally, the turtle is repositioned at (x, y).

That just leaves position:

```
position(x, y)
int x, y;
{
        x_turtle = x << 8;
        y_turtle = y << 8;
        if (writing)
                point(x, y);
}
```

That's simple enough; the new x_turtle and y_turtle values become 256 times x and y respectively and a point is plotted at (x, y) if the pen is down.

Incidentally, you'll have noticed that throughout I have shifted 8 bits left or right rather than multiply or divide by 256. Obviously this speeds things up, but there is a possible problem, which we'll encounter again in Chapter 16. It's this: when a right shift occurs on an int the sign bit *should* be propagated leftwards so that the sign of the result is unchanged. Normally this does happen, and there's no problem; but on some C compilers a right shift is implemented as a logical shift (so that zero's are used to fill on the left regardless of sign) whatever the type of the variable being shifted. It's easy to get round this problem if it exists; simply see the graph space as first quadrant only, so that all x, y values are positive. This may well be the way your library graphics functions work anyway in which case it's easiest to keep to this convention. For consistency, positional variables should then be unsigned (x, y, x_turtle and y_turtle) but angle and distance variables remain as ints because they can go negative.

Turtle Incorporated

So far we have a pile of turtle functions that could be simply written into any program that uses them. That would be laborious and inconvenient; certainly not in keeping with the C philosophy! Most C compilers provide no fewer than three ways to do the job more elegantly:

1. *Use the #include preprocessor command.* Create a file containing all the turtle functions called, say, 'turtle.c'. Now precede any turtle graphics program with:

$$\#\text{include } \langle \text{turtle}.c \rangle$$

and, of course, all the functions are included prior to compilation.

There is one disadvantage to this. Since all the functions are included, they will all be compiled, even though they may not all be called. As a result the object code may be bigger than necessary, although in this example, with only a few small functions, it's unlikely to matter much.

2. *Modify the standard library.* You could append the new functions to the source code of the standard library and recompile it. That way the turtle graphics commands become part of the language. Of course, you should be sure the code is bug-free before doing this; having suspect library functions is not to be recommended.

   Some compilers have librarian utilities that allow compiled functions to be added to the compiled version of the library. That saves a fairly long-winded recompilation, but the effect is the same.

3. *Use the linker.* Finally you could make more use of the linker than we have so far. I've simply said that it will link compiled functions from the standard library, but it's usually more sophisticated than that. It will link functions from *any* compiled file provided that file is specified as an argument at link time. The linker may even tell you, if it has been unsuccessful in finding a function, what the function is, and give you the option of specifying another file to search for it. The precise details are implementation dependent.

Finally in this chapter, I'll show how our turtle's course can be made less erratic, or anyway more accurate, by employing float.

Seeketh after a Sine

The usual way to compute special functions, such as SIN, COS, etc., is to *approximate* them by something easier, for example a polynomial, or a quotient p/q of two polynomials (known as a *rational function*). An entire branch of mathematics, known as *approximation theory*, is devoted to just this task.

Probably the first idea that springs to mind is to approximate SIN(x) by the front end of its *Taylor series*:

$$x - x^3/6 + x^5/120 - x^7/5040 + \cdots$$

Like most things that first spring to mind, this is not necessarily the best idea. Other approximations can provide more accuracy for less work. But it does have some advantages, which make it worth looking into.

Let's take the series up to the x^5 term only, and rearrange it in the form:

$$((x^2/5.4 - 1)x^2/3.2 + 1)x \tag{*}$$

(This process is called *nesting*.) Here's a simple C routine to implement it:

```
sintayl(x)
float x;
{
    float y;
    y = x * x;
    return (((0.05*y - 1) * 0.166667*y + 1) * x);
}
```

TABLE 15.2. Comparison of the
sine function with its Taylor series
to order 5, and its Padé
approximation, $f(x)$

x	$\sin(x)$	Taylor: $\mathrm{sintayl}(x)$	Padé $f(x)$
0	.0000	.0000	.0000
.1	.0998	.0998	.0998
.2	.1987	.1987	.1987
.3	.2955	.2955	.2955
.4	.3894	.3894	.3894
.5	.4794	.4794	.4794
.6	.5646	.5646	.5646
.7	.6442	.6442	.6442
.8	.7174	.7174	.7173
.9	.7833	.7833	.7832
1.0	.8414	.8416	.8413
1.1	.8912	.8916	.8908
1.2	.9320	.9327	.9313
1.3	.9635	.9648	.9624
1.4	.9854	.9874	.9834
1.5	.9975	1.0007	.9944
1.6	.9996	1.0007	.9948

Table 15.2 shows how sin and sintayl compare, for $0 < x < 1.6$ (the usual range $[0, 1]$). The range $-1.6 < x < 0$ is the same, but both SIN and sintayl have minus signs. (You can verify this with a BASIC program on your own machine.)

So to 4 decimal places, sintayl is an excellent approximation in the range $[0, 1]$, hence also $[-1, 1]$; and to 3 decimal places it's fine over the whole range $[-\pi/2, \pi/2]$.

You can easily see that the Taylor series is a much better approximation for x near 0 than it is for x large. The result is that by the time the series is accurate for x near 1 (say), it's unnecessarily accurate for x near 0. So a lot of the work of computation is wasted. However, the formula (∗) above is very simple anyway.

Another approximation is the rational function:

$$(60x - 7x^3)/(60 + 3x^2) = f(x), \text{ say,}$$

which is also a close approximation to $\sin(x)$ for $-\pi/2 < x < \pi/2$ (again see Table 15.2). Here x is measured in *radians*. It has often pleasant properties as well: it satisfies

$$f(-x) = -f(x)$$
$$f(0) = 0$$

just as sin does. And the denominator $60 + 3x^2$ is never zero. The function

$f(x)$ arises by a technique called *Padé approximation*, in case you're interested; and there's a *vast* theory about that.

   This leaves us with two minor problems, other than actually writing the code:

(a) Convert from degrees to radians.
(b) Deal with angles outside the range, where either function above rapidly becomes a very *bad* approximation to sin(x).

For the first, note that:

$$x \text{ degrees} = x/180 \text{ radians},$$
$$\pi \text{ is very close to } 355/113.$$

In fact $355/113 = 3.141593 =$ to 6 decimal places. So x degrees $\simeq$ $355x/(113*180) = 71x/(113*36)$ radians. Thinking of this as:

$$x/36 * 71/113$$

we retain accuracy as long as possible. For instance, suppose $x = 45°$, a typical size. Then

$$x/36 \simeq 1.25$$
$$-x/36 * 71 \simeq 89$$
$$x/36 * 71/113 \simeq 0.78.$$

   The second is dealt with by a technique called (rather pretentiously) *range-reduction*, which we used in writing *isin* and *icos* above. Thinking in degrees (an advantage here since 360 is an integer but 2π isn't!), we have two useful facts:

(1) $\sin(x + 360k) = \sin(x)$
(2) $\sin(180 - x) = \sin(x)$

See Figure 15.2.

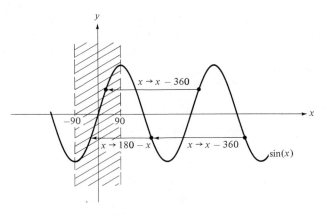

FIGURE 15.2. Range-reduction for sin(x).

Using (1) we can bring x into the range $[0, 360]$, or better, $[-90, 270]$. Then using (2) we can bring x into the range $[-90, 90]$ for which $f(x)$ is a good approximation.

A Trig Suite in C

We can now write a sine routine in C. First we assume x in the range $[-90, 90]$:

```
sintayl(x)
float x;
{
    float y;
    x = x / 36 * 71 / 113;
    y = x * x;
    return (((0.5*y - 1) * .166667*y + 1) * x);
}
```

Now suppose x is (possibly) not in this range. Then we can either add (or subtract) multiples of 360 to get it into the range $[-90, 270]$; and then use the results above to reduce to $[-90, 90]$. Here's what you get:

```
sin(x)
float x;
{
    while (x < -90)
        x += 360;
    while (x > 270)
        x -= 360;
    return sintayl(x);
}
```

What about the cosine? Well, we *could* start with a Padé approximation to $\cos(x)$, and follow the same lines. But there's an easier way, because (as we've seen in the integer case)

$$\cos(x) = \sin(90 - x)$$

for x in degrees. So all we need is

```
cos(x)
float x;
{
    return sin(90 - x);
}
```

PROJECT

Write C functions to compute (approximately!) the trigonometric functions:

$$\tan x \,(= \sin x/\cos x)$$
$$\cot x \,(= \cos x/\sin x)$$
$$\sec x \,(= 1/\cos x)$$
$$\operatorname{cosec} x \,(= 1/\sin x)$$

Make these return very large values when the denominator vanishes (rather than try to divide by zero!) and set a suitable overflow flag as a warning that this has occurred.

CHAPTER 16

... and Using Them

"Would you like to see a little of it?" said the Mock Turtle.
  "Very much indeed," said Alice.
  "Come, let's try the first figure!" said the Mock Turtle to the Gryphon.
"We can do it without lobsters, you know. Which shall sing?"

Alice's Adventures in Wonderland

Now comes the fun: mobilizing our faithful turtle in pursuit of art, science, and technological know-how. I've written this Chapter assuming the unsophisticated Integer Turtle Graphics is in use; but apart from changes to the type of variables and the standard initialization, the same programs will work with higher-precision Turtle Graphics.

I'll also assume that you will "#include" our existing Turtle package, so that the existing global definitions are always available.

As each new Turtle Graphics function is written, you can add it to this file. So we'll build up an ever-more flexible range of commands.

Topics covered include rectangles, ordinary or tilted polygons, circles, stars, spirals (and squirals), and as the *pièce de resistance*, the Koch snowflake curve.

But the real advantage of Turtle Graphics is that you can easily produce your *own* creative designs, without having to think about the mechanism whereby the computer produces them on the screen.

Rectangles

First, let's write four standard commands:

```
left(dist)
int dist;
{
    turnto(180);
    move(dist);
}
right(dist)
int dist;
{
    turnto(0);
    move(dist);
}
up(dist)
int dist;
{
    turnto(90);
    move(dist);
}
down(dist)
int dist;
{
    turnto(270);
    move(dist);
}
```

These are pretty much self-explanatory!

Next, a function to draw a rectangle of given *height* and *width*, whose lower left corner is at the current turtle position:

```
rectangle(height, width)
int height, width;
{
    turnto(0);
    right(width);
    up(height);
    left(width);
```

```
                    down(height);
        }
```

I'd like you to generalize this a shade.

Problem 1

Write a function tiltrec(height, width, angle) which produces a tilted rectangle as in Figure 16.1.

Try this problem now, because I'm going to use the answer. (Look it up if—heaven forbid—you have trouble.)

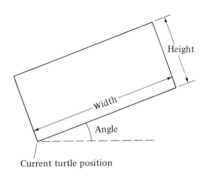

Current turtle position

FIGURE 16.1. Data for *tiltrec*.

Fan-Dancing

We can assemble tilted rectangles to make windmills, fans, propellers, and their ilk. See Figure 16.2.

A single multi-variable routine will do it.

```
fan(sang, iang, num, height, width)
                                    └──────── width of blade
                                    ───────── height of blade
                                    ───────── number of blades
                                    ───────── angle between blades
                                    ───────── start angle
```

Here it is.

```
        fan(sang, iang, num, height, width)
        int sang, iang, num, height, width;
        {
              int n, a;
              a = sang;
              for (n = 0; n < num; n++) {
                    tiltrec(height, width, a);
```

$$a \mathrel{+}= \text{iang};$$
$$\}$$
$$\}$$

You may prefer a variant.

        fan2(sang, iang, fang, height, width)

                               └——————————— finish angle

like this.

```
fan2(sang, iang, fang, height, width)
int sang, iang, fang, height, width;
{
        int a;
        for (a = sang; a <= fang; a += iang)
                tiltrec(height, width, a);
}
```

To get the pictures in Figure 16.2 you must write main programs that call

(a) fan(45, 90, 4, 20, 40)
(b) fan(45, 10, 10, 5, 40)
(c) fan(0, 45, 8, 20, 30)

respectively.

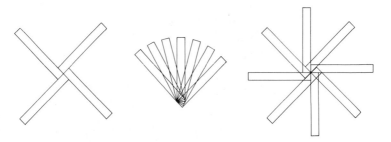

FIGURE 16.2. Tilting at windmills.

Problem 2

Do this. For something fancier, try

```
main()
{
        int k;
        initialize();
        for (k = 0; k < 8; k++) {
                turnto(0);
                move(10);
```

```
            pendown();
            fan(30, 5, 24, 60, 4);
            penup();
        }
    }
```

Polygons

It's very easy to draw an *n*-sided regular polygon whose side has length *d*:

```
            polygon(n, d)
            int n, d;
            {
                int t = 0;
                while (t++ <= n) {
                    move(d);
                    turn(360 / n);
                }
            }
```

Note that since *t* is incremented before the test we need $<=$ rather than $<$. It's then possible to produce some quite attractive results, for example

```
            main()
            {
                int d;
                initialize();
                for(d = 10; d < 100; d += 10)
                    polygon(5, d);
            }
```

However, with polygons it's often more useful to know what the *centre* and *radius* is. This is by no means obvious in the above format (see Fig. 16.3). We can work out how to define *d* in terms of *r*, and how to produce the correct

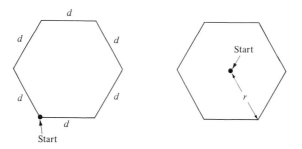

FIGURE 16.3. Free-form and centred polygons.

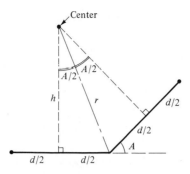

FIGURE 16.4. Calculations for a centred polygon.

offset for the centre, by using a bit of trigonometry on Figure 16.4, which represents two consecutive sides of a rectangular n-gon. (If trig isn't your bag, ignore the next few paragraphs of theory and go straight to the program.)

We have:

$$\sin(A/2) = (d/2)/r,$$
$$\cos(A/2) = h/r$$

Here:

$$A = 360/n \quad \text{so} \quad A/2 = 180/n.$$

So:

$$d = 2r\sin(A/2)$$
$$= r * 256\sin(A/2)/128$$
$$= r * s[180/n]/128$$

Similarly:

$$h = r * s[90 - 180/n]/256$$

since $\cos(x) = \sin(90 - x)$. Therefore the required code is:

```
centpoly(n, r)
int n, r;
{
    in d;
    d = r * s[180/n]/128;
    penup();
    turnto(-90);
    move(r * s[90 - 180/n]/256);
    turn(-90);
    move(d/2);
    turn(180);
    pendown();
    polygon(n, d);
}
```

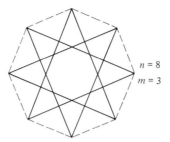

FIGURE 16.5. A star.

So, for some concentric heptagons, you could write

```
main()
{
        int k;
        initialize();
        for (k = 0; k < 10; k += 5) {
                centpoly(7, 10 * k);
                position(0, 0);
        }
}
```

Circle

You can get a pretty good approximation to a circle by using (say) a 30-gon. So

$$polygon(30, r)$$

is a 'circle' radius r. If r is big, you may need to increase the 30.

Stars

If you take the vertices of an n-sided polygon and join those that are m edges apart, you get a star as in Figure 16.5.

Problem 3

Write a function star (n, m) to implement this idea. *Hint*: the angle to be *turned* through is now $m * 360 / n$, otherwise it's just as for a polygon.

Spirals

If we perform a long series of *moves* and *turns*, and slowly increase the distance, or tinker with the angle, then typically we get a polygonal spiral. Here's a

FIGURE 16.6. Spyral (40, 10, 1, 90) gives a squiral.

general function along these lines:

```
spyral(num, sd, inc, angle)
int num, sd, inc, angle;
{
        while (num-- >= 0) {
                move(sd);
                turn(angle);
                sd += inc;
        }
}
```

For example:

```
spyral(40, 10, 1, 90);
```

produces a square spiral (*squiral*) as in Figure 16.6.

Change the angle to something close to 90°, but not quite (say 88° or 92°) and the corners will themselves appear to spiral.

Problem 4

Can you write a recursive function to produce squirals?

The Koch Snowflake

Finally, something more advanced. Around the turn of the century, Helge von Koch invented a curve called the *snowflake* to show that an infinitely long curve can enclose a finite area. It starts with an equilateral triangle and repeatedly modifies it by adding triangular peaks in the middle of each side.

There are various ways of drawing the snowflake. I'm going to use one that develops a string holding a long sequence of left and right turn symbols "*l*" or "*r*". The first generation is:

"*lll*"

(three consecutive lefts—a triangle) followed by:

"*lrlrlrlrlrlr*"

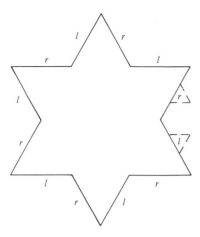

FIGURE 16.7. Adding a bump to the side of the snowflake: each "*l*" becomes "*lrlr*", and each "*r*" becomes "*rrlr*".

(a Star of David). Successive generations are obtained by replacing each "*l*" with a sequence "*lrlr*", and each "*r*" by "*rrlr*". See Figure 16.7.

One minor point to settle before we start. The string of *l*'s and *r*'s will be called *snow*; and we'll need a temporary area *temp* to manipulate it. How long should these strings be?

Well, *snow* quadruples in length each generation. So we have

$$
\begin{array}{llr}
\text{generation 1} : \text{length} & 3 \\
\text{\textquotedbl} \qquad 2 : \text{\textquotedbl} & 12 \\
\text{\textquotedbl} \qquad 3 : \text{\textquotedbl} & 48 \\
\text{\textquotedbl} \qquad 4 : \text{\textquotedbl} & 192 \\
\text{\textquotedbl} \qquad 5 : \text{\textquotedbl} & 768
\end{array}
$$

So two arrays of 800 bytes each will be more than adequate.

Here's the actual program:

```
char snow[800], temp[800];
main()
{
    int gen, d;
    initialize();
    printf("Enter side length");
    scanf("%d", &d);
    strcpy(snow, "lll");
    for (gen = 0; gen < 5; gen++) {
        position(50, 50);
        turnto(-120);
        if (gen > 0)
```

```
                    iterate();
                  display(d);
                  pause(DELAY);
           }
    }
```

Here *pause*, *iterate*, and *display* are three new functions. *pause* is just a time-delay. For instance:

```
              pause (t)
              int t;
              {
                  while(t--)
                    ;
              }
```

DELAY can be set up in a #define statement to give a suitable interval between displays.
　　The string-handling is done by *iterate*:

```
         iterate()
         {
             int k = 0;
             strcpy(temp, "");
             while (snow[k])
                 if (snow[k++] == 'l')
                     strcat(temp, "lrlr");
                 else
                     strcat(temp, "rrlr");
             strcpy(snow, temp);
         }
```

Finally the *display* routine:

```
         display(d)
         int d;
         {
             int k = 0;
             clearscreen();
             while (snow[k]) {
                 if (snow[k++] == 'l')
                     turn(120);
                 else
                     turn(-60);
                 move (d);
             }
         }
```

Here clearscreen() is whatever you need to do to get the screen clear—possibly *printf* some control character. Or a suitable function may be in the library.

Afterthoughts...

This is only the beginning. If you've got this far you'll have no trouble expanding the range of abilities of your home-bred Turtle Graphics. And you can tailor your Turtle to your personal prerequisites, thanks to the enormous flexibility of C.

And all this is just one example of how, by writing a suite of C functions, you can enhance the native abilities of your computer. It's not hard to think of others—a geometry kit for the mathematically minded, with functions

ruler (one-point, another-point)
protractor(angle)

and the like; or a musical suite with functions ranging from

allegretto( )

to

brandenburg_concerto( )

A veritable Symphony in C!

Answers

Problem 1

```
tiltrec(height, width, angle)
int height, width, angle;
{
    int t;
    turnto(angle);
    for (t = 0; t < 2; t++) {
        move(width);
        turn(90);
        move(height);
        turn(90);
    }
}
```

Note that the turtle ends facing in the direction *angle*.

Problem 2

(a)

```
main()
{
    initialize();
    fan(45, 90, 4, 20, 40);
}
```

(b, c) replace the parameters in *fan* with the correct values: leave the rest unchanged.

Problem 3

```
star(n, m, d)
int n, m, d;
    {
        int t = 0;
        while (t++ <= n) {
            move(d);
            turn(360 * m / n);
        }
    }
```

I won't bore you with the 'centred' version, but here's another hint if you want to write one yourself: Centre the surrounding *n*-gon and then *turn* a suitable angle before calling *star*.

Problem 4

```
squiral(num, sd, inc)
int num, sd, inc;
    {
        move(sd);
        turn(90);
        sd += inc;
        if (num--)
            squiral(num, sd, inc);
    }
```

PROJECT

If you tried *polygon* using a number of sides that do not divide 360° exactly, you probably found that it does not quite join up correctly. Clearly this is because the integer division loses a remainder and such errors build up quite noticeably for a large number of sides.

Can you improve the situation by checking remainders on *all* divisions (including the shift right operations) and performing appropriate round-ups?

CHAPTER 17

Random Thoughts

The confusion got worse every moment.

Through the Looking Glass

As any programmer knows, random numbers can be extremely useful animals, particularly in simulations and games programs. And, of course, it's a simple matter to get hold of them; simply use a function called RND or rand or random which produces them between zero and one, or between limits you define, like rabbits out of a hat. Your C library almost certainly has at least one function that does the job for you.

But have you ever stopped to wonder, when using them with gay abandon, just *how* random they are? Or what the question "How good is a random number generator?" actually means? No? Well, now's your chance.

Some Basic Ideas

In fact, no digital computer produces sequences of random numbers. At least, that statement is true if we chose to define such a sequence as a set of numbers $r_0, r_1, r_2, r_3 \ldots$ such that if we know r_p, there is no possible way of predicting the next number, r_{p+1}. All conventional random number generators perform a sequence of (surprisingly simple) arithmetic operations on r_p to produce r_{p+1}, so if you know the formula, the prediction is trivial. Generally such generators are said to produce pseudo-random numbers for this reason.

A commonly used technique is the linear congruential generator, which adopts the following deceptively simple relationship

$$r_{p+1} = (ar_p + c) \bmod m$$

a and c are constants and the mod operation has the effect of generating the remainder after the contents of the bracket have been divided by m. So if a, c and m are global variables, or the subject of #define statements, a C random number function might appear as

```
maybe_random()
{
    r=(a*r + c)%m;
    return r;
}
```

Of course, r would have to be a global variable, because its previous value has to be retained between calls. Alternatively, it could be a local static, if your compiler allows this.

It's clear that arbitrarily chosen values of a, c and m are unlikely to give a random sequence. For example, if $a = 4$, $c = 2$ and $m = 6$, then starting with $r = 1$ gives the sequence:

r	
1	$(4*1+2)\%6 = 0$
0	$(4*0+2)\%6 = 2$
2	$(4*2+2)\%6 = 4$
4	$(4*4+2)\%6 = 0$

From then on, the sequence 0, 2, 4 repeats indefinitely so that the numbers 3 and 5 can never be generated. We have a model of a rather heavily weighted die! Of course, even if this had generated a sequence like 1, 0, 2, 3, 5, 4 it must *then* repeat and we would have the odd concept of a die which, on any six throws, behaves apparently normally (except that two successive throws of the same value never happen) but which can then remember and repeat its previous six throws unerringly. This problem is easily dealt with. Simply choose a very large value of m so that the nonrepeating sequence is extremely long, and then partition *that* into the 6 groups representing the die throws.

Now members of a group may occur repeatedly without the whole sequence cycling.

However, if m is going to be large (a few million, say) it's going to get tricky to keep an eye on how the sequence is behaving. Let's keep m small for the minute while we're examining some of the problems.

O.K. $a = 4$, $c = 2$ didn't work; let's try $a = 1$, $c = 1$. We'll get:

r

1	$(1*1+1)\%6 = 2$
2	$(1*2+1)\%6 = 3$
3	$(1*3+1)\%6 = 4$
4	$(1*4+1)\%6 = 5$
5	$(1*5+1)\%6 = 0$
0	$(1*0+1)\%6 = 1$

That generates the whole sequence all right, but it's hardly random!

So we've identified two major problems. First, how do we ensure that the sequence generated contains every value (we say such a sequence has maximum length, and call it an m-sequence, for short)? Second, how do we know there aren't some hidden connections between the numbers in the sequence, even if not as blatant as the one above?

In a book entitled *Semi-numerical Algorithms* which is Volume II of *The Art of Computer Programming* (published by Addison-Wesley), Donald Knuth gives some relationships between a, c and m that are guaranteed to provide m-sequences. I shall not reproduce them here, but rather encourage you to delve into this volume for yourself, since it is a source of instruction, amusement, and facination. Knuth devotes more than one hundred pages to this topic alone.

Testing "Randomness"

He also investigates a number of techniques for testing how "random" a particular sequence is (and remarks in passing that more time easily can be spent on such tests than in devising generators in the first place).

With this in mind, I shall restrict myself to just one type of test, which strikes me as particularly satisfying. The idea is this: we are aiming for a situation in which, in general, there is no connection between r_p and r_{p+1}. So let's assume that they *are* related. For example we could treat them as a coordinate pair (x, y) and then represent all such pairs on a graph. For our suspect sequence 1, 2, 3, 4, 5, 0 this would give:

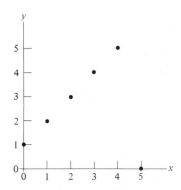

and the pattern is immediately obvious, indicating the lack of randomness. However, if a particular sequence passed this test by showing no particular pattern we cannot leave it at that, because there should be no discernible relationship between r_p and r_{p+2}, so we should repeat the process taking alternate values as the x, y pairs. Similarly, every third value should be extracted, then every fourth, and so on. In a sequence of a million numbers we're going to end up with a lot of graphs!

The Numerical Connection

Even if we do draw (or, more sensibly, get the computer to draw) all these scatter diagrams, how can we be sure that our subjective view is true, and that there is no discernible pattern in any of them? Clearly we need some good solid measure of the degree of correlation between any two sets of values.

Let's analyze the problem slightly differently. Suppose the sequence of numbers being generated represents the random noise that's always present in a hi-fi amplifier or (more noticeably) radio, even when there's no signal present. The average value of this noise is zero; in other words, its value is equally likely to go positive or negative. That's easily modelled—simply subtract the average value of the sequence from each number so that 4, 3, 0, 2, 1, 5 becomes 1.5, 0.5, −2.5, −0.5, −1.5, 2.5 for instance.

Now look at two copies of this sequence:

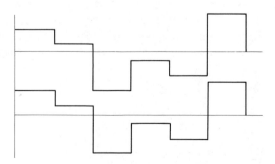

Suppose we multiply together the two values at each time interval, and add the results:

$$
\begin{array}{rcrcr}
1.5 & \times & 1.5 & = & 2.25 \\
0.5 & \times & 0.5 & = & 0.25 \\
-2.5 & \times & -2.5 & = & 6.25 \\
-0.5 & \times & -0.5 & = & 0.25 \\
-1.5 & \times & -1.5 & = & 2.25 \\
2.5 & \times & 2.5 & = & 6.25 \\
\hline
 & & & & 17.5
\end{array}
$$

Obviously we get a positive result because we've been squaring numbers, so that their signs have no significance. If the sequence had been very long, this result would get very large quite quickly. However, if we *delay* the second signal by one time interval (and treat the sequence cyclically, since we know that's the way it is in practice) this happens:

$$
\begin{array}{rcrcr}
1.5 & \times & 2.5 & = & 3.75 \\
0.5 & \times & 1.5 & = & 0.75 \\
-2.5 & \times & 0.5 & = & -1.25 \\
-0.5 & \times & -2.5 & = & 1.25 \\
-1.5 & \times & -0.5 & = & 0.75 \\
2.5 & \times & -1.5 & = & -3.75 \\
\hline
 & & & & 1.5
\end{array}
$$

Now, of course, some negative results *are* possible, and if the sequence really is random, they're just as likely as positive results, so the whole thing should cancel out to zero, or as near as makes no difference. This "delay" is equivalent to our previous analysis of comparing successive values in the sequence. Choose a delay of two time intervals and that's equivalent to comparing alternative values, and so on. Expressing this mathematically we're evaluating:

$$A(d) = \sum_t r(t).r(t+d)$$

where $r(t)$ is the random number generated at time t and $r(t+d)$ is that generated d time intervals later. The idea is that this sum ought to be close to zero for all values of d except zero. So if we were to graph the function for all values of d we would get something like:

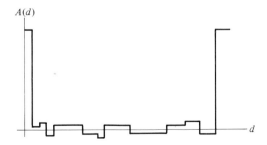

The second peak will occur when *d* is equal to the cycle length, at which point we're back to square one.

$A(d)$ is a close relative of an animal called the autocorrelation function, should you wish to know.

Notice, incidentally, that I'm not saying that $A(d)$ should be *exactly* zero for all non-zero values of *d*. As Knuth remarks, that would be suspiciously *too* neat; the *unpredictability* would have become predictable! That leaves us with the question "Just *how* close to zero is close enough?" There's no simple answer to that, except to say that it should be small compared with the peak value at $d = 0$.

Problem 1

Write a C program to evaluate A(d) for the first 200 numbers in the library random number function (i.e., assume that the whole sequence is only 200 numbers long—if you evaluate the complete sequence, you'll be at it forever).

Linear Feedback Shift Registers

There are two major problems with the linear congruential generation technique. First, the production of each number involves a multiplication, an addition and a division (to get the remainder). That makes it slow, which is bad news in this context because almost any program using random numbers is going to repeat its operations many times to get a clear idea of what is happening on average. After all, if you toss a coin six times and it comes down heads on each occasion you don't immediately jump to the conclusion that this will always happen; you repeat the experiment. The second problem has just been highlighted: if you've got a sequence that is sufficiently long to be useful, it's going to take far too long to test it exhaustively for randomness.

Here's a second approach that can be made to deal with both those problems. Imagine we have a register from which bits can be extracted and combined using logical operations. Suppose further that the register is then shifted right one bit, and the bit output from the sequence of logical operations is used to fill the senior bit of the register, like this:

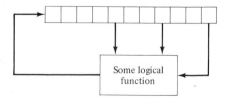

Clearly, we could produce a sequence of numbers this way. But would it be random? The answer is yes, under certain conditions. First, all the operations have to be XOR. Second, zero must never be generated (why?). The third problem is to ensure that an *m*-sequence is generated. Only certain positions for the XOR operations will do this, and there is a body of mathematical theory, which is too complex to go into here, which allows you to determine ideal positions for them. More importantly from our point of view, the mathematics proves that, provided we manage to choose a configuration which *does* generate an *m*-sequence, it is guaranteed to have a near ideal autocorrelation function.

Let's look at a simple example:

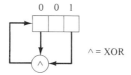

Here there's only one XOR operation performed on the senior and junior bits of a 3-bit word. With the seed as shown the first feedback digit is $0 \wedge 1 = 1$ so we get 100. The complete sequence becomes:

001	feedback digit	= 1
100		1
110		1
111		0
011		1
101		0
010		0
001		

and then it starts repeating. Since zero can't occur, that *is* an *m*-sequence. I leave it to you to check the autocorrelation function.

It's now clear why this is an interesting organization in terms of C programming, because it uses the machine level operations XOR, SHIFT and (by implication) AND for masking. Of course, all those operations are directly available to the C programmer. So the result should be pretty quick.

A Practical Program

Since I haven't explained the mathematical background, we shall have to investigate possible configurations by trial and error. (Even if I had done so, it's still necessary to do a fair bit of tinkering.)

We'll start by assuming that we're restricted to a 16-bit word, and that we can enter the positions of the bits to be sampled. For instance, to model this register:

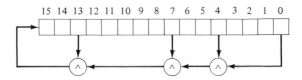

we enter 0, 4, 7, 13. These data will be used to set up an array of appropriate masks. The array will be global, for simplicity. Then the random number generator will be called 65536 times. Every result will be compared with the seed. If the first recurrence of the seed is the 65536th value we have an *m*-sequence. If the seed has not recurred at all by this time, the sequence must be looping on some other value or group of values, so it's no good to us. Simple isn't it?

```
int masks [10];
unsigned reg = 1;
main()
{
    char in_string[40];
    unsigned n;
    printf("Enter bit positions, separated by colons");
    scanf("%s", in_string);
    set_masks(in_string);
    for (n = 1; n < 65535; n++) {
        rng();
        if (reg == 1) {
            printf("Sequence length is %d", n);
            exit(0);
        }
    }
    rng();
    if (reg == 1)
        printf("m-sequence!!");
}
```

So main calls two functions; set_masks that will set up the masks array, and rng which evaluates the next number in the sequence from the current value in the global variable reg and replaces it. Notice that reg is unsigned. I'll explain why later.

```
set_masks(p)
char *p;
{
    int i = 0;
    strcat(p, ":");
    while (*p) {
```

```
            masks[i++] = 1 << atoi(p);
            while(*p++ != ':')
                    ;
        }
        masks[i] = 0;
}
```

The string passed to set_masks consists, remember, of a set of numbers separated by colons, like this, for instance:

$$0:7:12:13$$

which indicates that there are feedback contributions from bits 0, 7, 12, and 13. You'll notice that the first thing I do is to concatenate an extra colon on to the string. This means that every number can be treated the same way, which leads to neater code. The outer while loop simply looks for the end of the string. As long as it hasn't been reached an element of masks is set to 1 shifted left a number of bits. For my example data, this number is zero to start with, because p initially points to 0, and atoi uses any non-digit (in this case the first colon) as a delimiter. The inner while moves the pointer to one character past the next colon, which will either be the next number to turn into a mask or a null, in which case the loop is exited, and the next element of masks is zeroed to signal the end of the feedback contributions.

All of which just leaves us with rng itself:

```
        rng()
        {
            int i = 0, fbit = 0;
            while (masks[i++])
                    fbit ^= select(masks[i - 1]);
            reg >>= 1;
            fbit <<= 15;
            reg |= fbit;
        }
```

There's nothing very remarkable here. The feedback bit (fbit) is evaluated by successively XORing with a value returned by a new function select which will select a bit from reg generated by the current mask and return zero or one depending on whether the result is zero or nonzero. reg is then shifted right to make way for the feedback bit. At this point I can explain why reg had to be declared as an unsigned. The problem is that a right shift on an int may, not unreasonably, be seen as a "divide by 2" operation. If this *is* so (and it isn't true for all C compilers) a bit pattern with a one in the senior bit position will be treated as negative, and so this bit must be filled with a one after the shift to preserve the sign. As far as we are concerned, it will be simpler if this bit is always zero, which is guaranteed to be the case if reg is unsigned.

Finally, reg is ORed with fbit (having first shifted fbit so that its value is in the most significant bit) so that the feedback is taken care of.

We haven't quite finished. There remains select.

```
select(mask)
int mask;
{
        if(reg & mask)
                return 1;
        return 0;

}
```

Problem 2

Use the above program (perhaps with modifications) to investigate the nature of number sequences generated by feedback shift registers. See if you can find a configuration which leads to an *m*-sequence.

Answers

Problem 1

```
#define MEANVAL 16284
int rn[200];
main()
{
        int n, d;
        float autoc();
        for (n = 0; n < 200; n++)
                rn[n] = rand() - MEANVAL;
        for (d = 1; d < 200; d++)
                printf("d=%d  a=%f\n", d, autoc(d));
}
autoc(d)
int d;
{
        float a = 0;
        int p;
        for (p = 0; p < 200; p++)
                a += rn[p]*rn[(p + d)%200];
        return a;

}
```

There are several assumptions implicit in this piece of code. First I'm guessing that the library random number function (which is assumed to be called rand) generates integers in the range 0–32767. Hence the definition of MEANVAL to be half this maximum, to make the value held in the array rn swing about zero when this is subtracted. Obviously you can alter this appropriately. Second I'm assuming you've got the float type available, because you're going to get some very large numbers when you do the multiplications. For the same reason I haven't bothered to evaluate the function at $d = 0$, because that's *guaranteed* to be massive, although with an appropriately generous float you might get away with it.

Problem 2

Several things should become apparent fairly quickly. First, bit 0 *has* to contribute to the feedback path. Otherwise the sequence must degenerate to zero immediately, since the only bit that is set drops off the right-hand end of the word and the feedback bit is zero. Second, there are other combinations that can lead to zero being generated, so it's worthwhile building in an appropriate test. Thirdly, you get longer sequences with an even number of bits contributing to the feedback path than with an odd number. Fourth, a small number of contributing bits is invariably bad news. This is no surprise; after all, it is then likely that there will be a large number of successive values that will just be the previous value divided by two as the shift right (and nothing else!) occurs. Thus you can't get a good autocorrelation function, and by implication, neither can you get an *m*-sequence.

I've found two configurations that give 16-bit *m*-sequences. The first requires contributions from bits

$$0:2:4:6:10:12:14:15$$

and the second uses bits

$$0:6:10:12:14:15$$

Obviously, the latter executes faster.

PROJECTS

1. Write random number generators using the above configurations. Obviously these can be optimized for speed now, since the masks no longer need to be variables. If your compiler implements bit fields (see Appendix 1) you don't even need masks, although it doesn't follow that the resulting code will be any faster.

   Compare the results with your library random number function. Are they quicker? Do they produce similar results in random number tests?

2. For simplicity, my code has assumed that the target machine has a 16-bit word. Strictly, this is bad practice. Ideally one should write C programs that are transportable between different machine architectures with only limited changes to #define statements which describe the changes in word length and so on. Rewrite the random number test routines to allow for any word length.

3. Revise the test routines to handle double length words (assuming you don't have the long type—we can't make things too easy, can we?).

"Would you tell me, please, which way I ought to go from here?"

"That depends a good deal on where you want to go," said the Cat.

"I don't much care where—" said Alice.

"Then it doesn't matter which way you go," said the Cat.

"—so long as I get somewhere," Alice added as an explanation.

"Oh, you're sure to do that," said the Cat, "if you only walk long enough."

Alice's Adventures in Wonderland

Loose Ends

*"You should have said," the Queen went on in a tone of grave reproof,
"'It's extremely kind of you to tell me all this.'"*

Through the Looking Glass

Throughout this book it has been our first priority to keep things simple.
Inevitably, this has meant that some topics have been ignored, or only touched
upon, in the interest of clarity. We partially redress this balance here by
describing briefly some of the more glaring omissions of the main text.

(a) Bit Fields

These provide an alternative mechanism to the conventional "mask and shift"
approach to the isolation of groups of bits within a word. An int can be broken
up into *fields* of bits using the structure notation. For instance

```
struct { unsigned parity    : 1;
         unsigned zone      : 3;
         unsigned numeric : 4;
       } byte;
```

defines an int called byte consisting of 1 bit called parity, a 3-bit field called zone, and a 4-bit field called numeric. Individual fields can now be referenced in the conventional way for structure members. For example

$$\text{if (!byte.parity) } \{\,..\,\}$$

or

$$\text{if (byte.numeric} < 10) \{\,..\,\}$$

(b) Cast Operator

Generally, the programmer need not concern himself with implicit type conversions. For example

```
float f;
int i = 3;
f = i;
```

causes an automatic integer to floating point conversion. However, there are occasions on which it is necessary to force a type change on a variable. This is called a *cast*. For example, $f = i$, above, could be written

$$f = (\text{float}) \, i;$$

In general the form

$$(\text{type}) \text{ expression}$$

forces *expression* to be converted to *type*.

(c) Comma Operator

A comma expression consists of two expressions separated by a comma

$$a, b$$

a and b are both evaluated and then a is discarded. For instance:

$$\text{for } (i = 0; i < 100; x[i] = 0, i{+}{+})$$

will initialize the array x to zeros independent of the body of the loop.

(d) Command-Line Arguments

Most operating system interfaces provide mechanisms by which arguments can be passed to a C program when it is invoked. If such arguments are expected, main must have two arguments called, by convention, argc and argv:

```
main(argc, argv)
int argc;
char *argv[];
{ :
    :
}
```

argc is the *argument count* (i.e., the number of arguments in the list). argv is a vector of pointers to strings. Each string is an argument.

For example, suppose that each function of a program contains a statement such as

```
if(trace)printf("Inside function x\n");
```

so that, if the flag *trace* is '1', an output such as

Inside function *a*
Inside function *c*
Inside function *a*
Inside function *x*

etc., is produced.

It would be convenient to turn the flag on or off from the command line, so that instead of writing

```
exec test (or whatever, to run the program test)
```

we write

```
exec test traceon
```

or

```
exec test traceoff.
```

The necessary code would be

```
int trace;
main(argc, argv)
int argc;
char *argv[];
{
    if (argc != 1) {
        printf("Invalid argument list\n");
        exit(0);
    }
    if (!strcmp(argv[1], "traceon"))
        trace = 1;
    else
        if (!strcmp(argv[1], "traceoff"))
```

```
                    trace = 0;
              else {
                    printf("Invalid argument\n");
                    exit(0);
              }
              ⋮
```

This checks that there is exactly one argument, and prints an error message otherwise. It then takes the obvious action if the argument is "traceon" or "traceoff" and complains if it is neither of these.

Clearly, if there are several arguments, argc can be used to determine the limit of a for loop searching through them in argv.

Usually argv[0] contains the program name, although in some systems it is undefined.

(e) extern

We have observed that a C program may consist of several separate source files that are separately compiled and combined at link time. Suppose that one file contains a global variable definition. Clearly, no other file may contain a definition for the same variable, since that would lead to a duplicate storage allocation. On the other hand, if there is *no* reference to it in a source file that uses it but does not contain its definition, the compiler will report an error.

Thus a mechanism is required which will inform the compiler that the definition of a variable occurs in another file. For example, if n is an int that is defined elsewhere, but referenced in the current file, we write

extern int n;

The extern keyword indicates to the compiler that the definition of n is elsewhere. Its *type* is declared here however, so that any problems associated with pointer increments or casts can be resolved.

(f) Function Pointers

Just as an array name is a pointer to the array, so a function name is a pointer to the function. Consequently it is possible to pass such pointers to a function which will then call other functions, depending on its parameter list.

A typical use for this might be in a search routine where the key may be numeric or a string. The search routine itself would start:

```
              search(key_comp, pkey)
              int (*key_comp) ();
              char *pkey;
              { :
                    if ((*key_comp)(pkey) == 0) {...}
                    ⋮
```

Thus key_comp is defined as a pointer to a function which returns an int. A pointer to the target key is also passed (the target key itself can't be, because its type is unknown at this stage). Defining it as a pointer to characters will handle both possibilities, although it is a little dangerous. See section (j) for a better technique.

Now two functions called strcmp and numcmp can be used (which return, say, zero on a match, +1 on key too low and −1 on key too high). numcmp would have to be written, but strcmp is a standard library function (see Appendix 2). Then search is called with

$$search(numcmp, \&n);$$

or .

$$search(strcmp, \text{``Fred Bloggs''});$$

for example.

Note that, in the calling routine, the declaration:

$$int\ numcmp(\ ), strcmp(\ );$$

is necessary, even though both functions return ints. Otherwise the compiler will complain they are undefined when it encounters them in the parameter list.

(g) Preprocessor Commands

(i) *Macros with arguments.* The #define preprocessor command may have arguments in the replacement text. Thus

$$\#\,define\ half(x)\qquad (x)/2$$

will replace half$(a - 3)$ with $(a - 3)/2$. (Note the use of brackets here to ensure that, whatever x is, it is treated as an entity.)

(ii) *#undef.* This can be used to force the preprocessor to forget a definition. For example

$$\#\,undef\ BUFSIZE$$

(iii) *#ifdef.* This allows conditional compilation. For example suppose that BUFSIZE may have been defined as 100 (perhaps in a #include file) and should be set to 256.

We could write:

```
#ifdef BUFSIZE
    #undef BUFSIZE
    #def BUFSIZE 256
#else
    #def BUFSIZE 256
#endif
```

Note the forms #else and #endif, whose meanings are self-evident. There is also the form

$$\#\text{ifndef ident}$$

Meaning "if ident is *not* defined", and

$$\#\text{if constant\_expression}$$

which will cause execution of what follows if constant_expression is non-zero.

(h) Scope Rules

The scope rules as indicated so far are slightly incomplete. In particular, it is possible to define a variable at the head of *any* block. If this is done, the variable's scope is restricted to that block and any prior definition of the same variable name is suspended until the end of the block. Thus

```
{
    int j = 1, x;
    for (x = 0; x < 99; x++) {
        int j = 0;
        j++;
    }
}
```

will leave the for loop with $j = 1$.

(i) sizeof

The sizeof operator gives the size (in bytes) of its operand. For example

```
int n;
n = sizeof(n);
```

would give $n = 2$ for a machine with an 8-bit byte and 16-bit int. (Although there is no formal connection, the de facto standard is that a byte is the size of a char.)

Clearly, the most obvious use of sizeof is in allocating space for complex structures.

(j) Unions

A union is a variable whose type is ambiguous; that is it may hold data of different types at different times. For example, the type of pkey in section (f) of this appendix may be a pointer to an int or a pointer to characters. The technique employed there of defining pkey as a pointer to characters in either case is adequate (although unsatisfying) for *referencing* the data since, if an int *is* pointed to, the system will just pick up the appropriate number of bytes, but it *can* be very dangerous. For instance 'pkey++' causes a one byte increment which is unlikely to be correct if pkey points to an int.

The syntax is based on that for structures

```
union key_type {
    int * pi;
    char * pc;
} pkey;
```

This declares pkey to be a pointer to an int or a pointer to characters. To distinguish between them, the dot notation is borrowed from the structure syntax. So

```
pkey.pi
```

and

```
pkey.pc
```

are used to refer to the individual members of the union.

Quick Reference Guide

While the Beaver confessed, with affectionate looks
  More eloquent even than tears,
It had learned in ten minutes far more than all books
  Would have taught it in seventy years.

The Hunting of the Snark

(1) Operators

(a) Unary

Operator	Meaning	Examples	Description
*	defines a pointer	$a = *p;$	a gets the object pointed to by p.
&	address of	$p = \&a;$	p gets the address of a.
$-$	negate	$b = -a;$	b gets minus a.
!	not	if $(b \mathrel{!=} 3)..$	if b not equal to $3..$
		$a = !r;$	if $r = 0$, $a = 1$ else $a = 0$.
~	1's complement	$a = \mathord{\sim}b;$	flip bits of b and transfer to a.
++	increment	$b++;$	add one to b.
		if $(s[i++] = \text{' '})$	compare $s[i]$ with 'space' and then update i.
		if $(s[++i] = \text{' '})$	update i and then compare $s[i]$ with space.
$--$	decrement	$b--;$	subtract one from b.

(b) Binary

Operator	Meaning	Examples	Description
*	multiply	$r = a * b;$	multiply a by b and place result in r.
/	divide	$r = a/b;$	divide a by b and place result in r.
%	remainder	$r = a \% b;$	divide a by b and place remainder in r.
+	add	$r = a + b;$	add a to b and place result in r.
$-$	subtract	$r = a - b;$	subtract b from a and place result in r.
<<	shift left	$r = a << 3;$	shift a left 3 bits and place result in r.
>>	shift right	$r = a >> 2;$	shift a right 2 bits and place result in r.
&	AND (bitwise)	$r = a \& b;$	the bit patterns of a and b are ANDed and the result placed in r.
$\wedge$	XOR	$r = a \wedge b;$	the bit patterns of a and b are XORed and the result placed in r.
|	OR (bitwise)	$r = a \mid b;$	the bit patterns of a and b are ORed and the result placed in r.
&&	AND (logical)	if $(a \mathrel{!=} 0 \;\&\&\; a < 5)$	if a isn't 0 and is less than $5..$
||	OR (logical)	if $(a < 3 \;\|\|\; a > 6)$	if a is less than 3 or greater than $6..$

Operator	Meaning	Examples	Description
$<$	less than	see above	
$<=$	less than or equal to	if $(a <= 120)$	if a is less than or equal to 120..
$>$	greater than	see above	
$>=$	greater than or equal to	see above	
$==$	is equal to	if $(q == r)$	if q is equal to r..
$?:$	conditional	$r = a?b:c;$	if a is non-zero $r = b$, else $r = c$.
,	comma operator	$r = i++, j;$	evaluates left to right and then discards left operand. Thus i is incremented and $r = j$.
$->$	pointer to structure	$p -> year$	points to a member of a structure (year) if p is a pointer to the structure.
.	member of structure	date.year	isolates a member (year) of a structure (date).

(c) Assignments

'$=$' is used to mean 'gets'.
It may be preceded by any binary operator.
For example, $a += 5;$ is equivalent to $a = a + 5;$
$\qquad\qquad a <<= 3;$ is equivalent to $a = a << 3;$

(2) Data Types

Type	Comments
char	Usually (but not necessarily) 8 bits.
int	Arithmetic is 2's complement. Qualifiers are short and long.
unsigned	Arithmetic is mod 2^n where n is the word length. Qualifiers are short and long.
float	Single precision floating point.
double	Double precision floating point.
struct	User defined pseudo-type.
union	Allows a variable to be multi-typed.
Examples:	
char cval, letter;	sets up 2 bytes labelled cval and letter.
int $i, j, k;$	sets up 3 words labelled i, j and k. Arithmetic will be 2's complement.
unsigned posval;	sets up a word labelled posval. Arithmetic will take no account of sign.
int $1a[10]$, ra$[5][7];$	sets up a 10 element linear array $1a$ (0–9) and a 5×7 2-D array ra.
char *cp;	cp is a pointer to characters.
int *ip$[50];$	ip is an array of pointers to integers.

Type	Comments
char **cip[20];	cip is an array of pointers to pointers to characters.
struct date {	sets up a structure containing 3 integers and a character array.
int day;	
int month;	
int year;	
char mname[3];	
};	
struct date birthdate;	defines birthdate as a structure of type date.
struct date holidays[25];	defines holidays as a 25 element array of structures of type date.

(3) Storage Classes

Class	Comment
auto	variable is local to the function in which it is defined.
static	variable may be local to the function in which it is defined, or to the source file at whose head it appears. In either event it is not destroyed between function invocations.
extern	variable is global.
register	variable is assigned to a register if possible.

(4) Statements

Simple statements are always terminated by ;

Compound statements are sequences of simple statements enclosed between
   { } and may appear anywhere simple statements may appear.

In the following 'ex$N$' and 'sN' denote 'expression' and 'statement' respectively
   and N is an arbitrary digit which may be null.

General Form	Example	Comments

if (ex)s	if (val > 3) {
	   r++;
	   flag = 1;
	 }
		s is executed if ex is true (non-zero).

if (ex)
   s1
 else
   s2
	if (b == 0)
	   p = r;
	 else
	   p += 2;
		if ex is true s1 is executed; otherwise s2 is obeyed.

while (ex)s	while (a[i]) {
	   i++;
	   j--;
	 }
		s is executed until ex becomes false. The test occurs *first*.

General Form	Example	Comments
do *s* while (ex)	do n += 2; while ($a[n]$)	*s* is executed until ex becomes false. The test occurs *last*.
for (ex1; ex2; ex3)*s*	for ($i = 1; i < 8; i++$) $p[i] = 0$;	ex1 sets the initial condition; *s* and ex3 are executed until ex2 is false.

switch (ex)*s*	switch(c) {
	   case -1: $v = 4$;
	             break;
	   case 0: $v = -2$;
	             break;
	   default: $n++$
	 }
		The value of ex determines the case at which *s* is *entered*. The rest of *s* is then obeyed until a break or return is encountered. default is optional.

break;	break;	causes termination of the smallest enclosing while, do, for or switch.
continue;	continue;	causes a branch to the end of the smallest enclosing while, do or for, *inside* the loop.
return ex;	return flag;	control is passed back to the calling function. ex is optional, but if it is present, the called function has its value.
goto label;	goto out;	transfers control to the statement labeled label.

(5) Preprocessor Directives

Directive	Comment
#include ⟨filename⟩	the file 'filename' is included with the source.
#define ident reptext	all subsequent references in the source file to 'ident' are replaced by 'reptext'.
#if cexp	allows conditional compilation if the constant expression cexp is true.
#ifdef ident	allows conditional compilation if ident is currently defined.
#else	else clause for #if and #ifdef.
#endif	closes #if or #ifdef.
#undef indent	undefines ident.

(6) Constants

(a) Integers

decimal—sequence of digits, no leading zero, e.g. 5729
octal   —sequence of digits with leading zero, e.g., 0571
hex   —sequence of digits with leading 0x, e.g., 0x5*fa*3

(b) Floats

nonexponent form—e.g., 321.85
exponent form   —e.g., 3.2185e2

(c) Characters

single characters are enclosed in single quotes: for example, ch = 'b';
sets the byte ch to ASCII b.
strings are enclosed in double quotes: e.g., "a message"
Certain characters have standard escape sequences:
new line: $\backslash n$ formfeed: $\backslash f$ tab:$\backslash t$ backslash: $\backslash \backslash$
backspace: $\backslash b$ quote: $\backslash$'   return: $\backslash r$
bit pattern: $\backslash ddd$ (where ddd is an octal number)

(7) Common Library Functions

Function	Comment
Standard I/O	
getchar()	returns a character from stdin
putchar(c)	writes the character c to stdout
File I/O	
fopen(name, mode)	opens file 'name' for reading if 'mode' is r, for writing if it is w, and for appending if mode is a. 'name' and 'mode' are both pointers to strings. A channel identifier is returned, or 0 on failure.
fclose(cid)	the channel cid is closed, after its buffer has been flushed.
getc(cid)	returns a character from channel cid or EOF at end of file.
putc(c, cid)	the character c is output to channel cid.
fflush(cid)	the buffer associated with cid is flushed.
unlink(filename)	deletes the file pointed to by 'filename'.
lseek(cid, offset, start)	positions the file pointer on channel cid to offset bytes from the start of the file if start = 0, from its current value if start = 1 and from the end of the file if start = 2.
Formatted I/O	
printf(str, arg1, arg2,...)	prints arg1, arg2 etc., to stdout in format specified by str.
fprintf(cid, str, arg1, arg2,...)	prints arg1, arg2 etc., to channel cid in format specified by str.
scanf(str, arg1, arg2,...)	reads data from stdin to locations whose *addresses* are specified by arg1, arg2 etc., in format specified by str.
fscanf(cid, str, arg1, arg2,...)	as scanf, but data is taken from channel cid.
Format Conversion	
atoi(str)	returns the integer equivalent to the string pointed at by str.
sprintf(buf, str, arg1, arg2,...)	as printf, but data is transferred to a buffer pointed to by buf.
sscanf(buf, str, arg1, arg2,...)	as scanf, but data is found in a buffer pointed to by buf.

Function	Comment
String Handling	
strcat(dest, source)	concatenates the string pointed to by source on to that pointed to by dest.
strcmp(str1, str2)	returns a negative integer, 0 or a positive integer depending on whether str1 is less than, equal to or greater than str2.
strcpy(dest, source)	copies the string pointed to by source to dest.
strlen(str)	returns the length of the string pointed to by str.
Character Classification	
isalpha(c)	returns true if c is an alphabetic character.
isdigit(c)	returns true if c is a digit.
islower(c)	returns true if c is lower case.
isupper(c)	returns true if c is upper case.
isspace(c)	returns true if c is space, tab, or newline.
Character Conversion	
tolower(c)	if c is upper case, returns lower case equivalent, else returns c.
toupper(c)	opposite of tolower.
Miscellaneous	
abs(n)	returns absolute value of integer n.
calloc(count, size)	allocates and zeros count*size bytes of memory. Returns a pointer to this block, or 0 if there is inadequate space.
cfree(p)	frees a block of memory allocated using calloc pointed to by p.
exit(state)	return control to the operating system. state is normally 0, but may be set to 1 to flag an error return.

Index